WRITING THE SKIES:

INSPIRATIONAL DEVOTIONAL STORIES ABOUT SEEING GOD IN THE SMALL THINGS...

AMY ELIZABETH PIKE

Scripture quotations marked (NIV) are taken from the Holy Bible, New International Version®, NIV®. Copyright © 1973, 1978, 1984, 2011 by Biblica, Inc.™ Used by permission of Zondervan. All rights reserved worldwide. www.zondervan.com The "NIV" and "New International Version" are trademarks registered in the United States Patent and Trademark Office by Biblica, Inc.™

The Holy Bible, King James Version. New York: Oxford Edition: 1769; King James Bible Online, 2008. www.kingjamesbibleonline.org

For ordering information or questions/comments, you can contact me at:
writtenintheskies320@gmail.com
www.facebook.com/writtenintheskies
Twitter: @amyepike

Cover design & image: Mark Pike
©2013 Amy Elizabeth Pike
ISBN-13: 978-0615932071
ISBN-10: 061593207X
All rights reserved.

DEDICATION

To all of my family and friends who encouraged me along the way, I think of you the way my daughter Krista told me she loved me when she was little — "I love you more than chocolate sauces."

To my Lord & Savior Jesus Christ, I thank you for those little winks you give me almost daily — the ways you say, "I love you, and I see you."

To my husband Mark, I thank you for your patience as I wrote at such late hours. I am also grateful for all the technical expertise you provided. Thank you for always believing in me. I am blessed to have you in my life!

To my beautiful daughter Krista, you are very talented in music and writing. I hope that you will enjoy these stories throughout your life and always remember Ephesians 3:20! Thank you for also featuring some of your photography throughout this book.

To my parents Barbara and Jerry Bruner, thank you for raising me in a Christian home. I also thank you for supporting me in my writing and helping me find verses and lyrics when I couldn't find them. Thanks to my daddy for sharing some of his stories too.

To my mother-in-law and father-in-law Clifford and Patricia Pike, thank you for answering those tough Bible questions that I have asked throughout the years. I also thank you for loving me like a daughter and for the many prayers that you have prayed.

A special thanks to my family and friends, whose stories are shared in many of these devotions. Thank you to the Crumbley family for allowing me to share your inspiring story and photo with others. I also want to thank my editors: Patricia Pike, Carla Crosby, and Mark Pike, for all the time you invested in my work!

With Much Love,
Amy Elizabeth Pike

CONTENTS

Skywriting 10
Old Love Letters 13
Hitting Butterflies 15
Living with the "Junkyard Dog" 17
Mail from Grandma 19
Keeping Watch 21
Tight Rein 23
Early Birds 25
Empty Dish 26
The Quilt 27
The Lost Bead 29
The Easter Chicks 30
Cake Batter 32
Flower Petals 33
Raccoon Eyes 34
Little Beggar 36
Big Ben 38
Building on the Sand 39
The Harvest Moon 40
The Candle 42
Praying Hands 43
Crab Killer! 45
Dead Bug 47
Cowbirds 48
The Mysterious Musician 50
Daily Bread 52
Baby Powder 54
The Grill – Under Construction 55
Crumb Snatcher! 57
The Bug 58
New Heart 59
The Blood Donation Bus 60
The Tasty Pink Purse! 62
"Insongnia" 64
The Pine Tree Cross 65
Mrs. Wren 66
Daddy's Little Helper 68
Grapes of Faith 70

The Crepe Myrtle	72
Calluses	73
Bundle of Flowers	75
Fireflies	76
Grilling Steaks	78
The Harmonica	80
Redhead	81
Forsaken!	82
Happy Duck	84
Lost Tracks	85
The Unexpected Visitor	87
The Curtain	88
Just One Strike!	89
One Man's Trash	91
In Perfect Harmony	93
A Little "Warm-up"	94
Take Your Shoes Off!	96
Queen of the Hill	97
Seven Cents	99
Crazy Suicidal Squirrel	100
The Pink Dress	102
The Creepy Hand	104
The Bearded Dragon	106
Paneled Houses	107
The Butterfly	108
No Pasture	109
The 71-Night Revival	110
Come and Dine	111
The Fallen Tree	112
Walking Partners	113
The Cicada	115
Moon Struck	117
The Doves	118
Stuck in the Mud	119
Scarlett, the Other Woman!	121
The Flying Ants	123
Pattern	125
The Garage Sale	126
The Oyster	127
True Love	128
Sweet Nectar	129

Title	Page
Telling Sentences	130
The Sprayed Cat	131
Sweet Tooth	133
The Blanket	134
The Big Oak	136
One Way Street	138
The Ball Thief	139
The Garden Snake	141
The Liberty Bell	143
The Great Find	144
Whispering with God	145
The Music Assignment	146
Worthless Treasures	148
Where's Paw-Paw?	149
The Sailboat	151
The Peacock	152
5k Training	153
The Plum Tree	155
Thirsty Birds	156
The Searchlights	157
Top of the Toolbox	158
Who's Bigger?	160
Right on Time	161
Traveller's Endurance	163
Peanut Butter & Ant Sandwich	165
The House on the Hill	167
When the Lights Go Out!	169
The Stool	172
The Window That Wasn't There	174
Tuned In	176
Daisy's Surgery	177
Seeds of Doubt	178
Lost Dog	179
The Strings Concert	181
The Dead Battery	183
The Animal-Print Sweater	185
Paid In Full	187
The Black Swan	189
The Calculator	191
The Sistine Chapel	193
The Movie Theater	195

The Red Bandana 197
The "Loss Prevention" Officer 199
The Snail 201
Skyscraper 203
Canary in a Coal Mine 205
Higher and Higher Still 206
The Kitty-Cuddlers 208
Lost Guitar Picks 210
The Safe Room 212
320 Power! 214
Georgia Thumpers 216
Locked Door! 218
The Coin Jewelry 220
The Gym Membership 222
R.I.P., Red! 223
The Open Book Test 225
The Egg Salad Mess 226
Love Bug Season 228
In the Palm of His Hand 229
The Cowbell 231
Geraldo's New Home 233
Conclusion 235
Works Cited 236

INTRODUCTION

I am not a pilot, nor is anyone else in my family. To be honest, most of the people in my family would be afraid to set foot inside an airplane. Many in my family believe like our family preacher used to say that "Jesus said, 'lo I am with you always' (Matthew 28:20, KJV), but he didn't say anything about flying high and in an airplane."

I'm so glad to know that Jesus is with us always, whether high or low, near or far! I'm sure you are wondering by now the reason for the image on the front of the book you are holding. Why an airplane drawing lines in the sky? It's the adventure I feel almost daily with my Lord – the many ways that He reveals Himself daily that many people overlook.

My journey began when I was 27 years old. I was raised in a Christian home and had loving parents who took me to church every week and taught me about the Christian faith. I became a Christian at a young age, but my life changed when I was 27 years old. My husband and I, with our five-month-old baby, were transferred to a new city and my world was turned upside down.

God intervened and showed me that I no longer could depend upon myself for happiness and contentment. He showed me a new way to live and a new excitement that I had never felt before. I would learn not only how to depend upon Him for provisions and strength in challenging times, but that I could have a friendship with Him that goes much deeper than two buddies chatting over a latte. He would show me His true heart in ways that were totally unimaginable. Through family, nature, friends, and pets, I would capture a little piece of God's heart that would send chills up my spine. I'm so glad you have decided to open this book and see God through my eyes. I hope that you will ask God to open your eyes so that you can see Him through everyday life too!

Now unto him that is able to do exceeding abundantly above all that we ask or think, according to the power that worketh in us, Unto him be glory in the church by Christ Jesus throughout all ages, world without end. Amen.
Ephesians 3:20-21, KJV

SKYWRITING

It was a beautiful day with no gray clouds in sight. I always thought the skies in South Florida seemed bluer than anywhere I'd ever been. I could just sit outside for hours watching the puffy clouds dance across the blue sky, and often I did.

On this day, I was driving when I saw something remarkable. It was written across the sky, almost as though the sky was a piece of paper and a story was being told. One word told the entire story, the reason for everything — the blue skies, the reason for the day, and the reason for the pilot who painted the sky! The word spelled "Jesus."

I could almost hold out my hand and touch this word because it seemed so small — or was it? Just so you know, things aren't always what they seem!

Skywriting is an art that many pilots enjoy. Words are created from vaporized fluid in the plane's exhaust system. According to *Skywriter.info*, "Each letter is about one mile long and two miles above you." *Skywriter.info* also adds that, "On a clear day, each letter can be seen from the ground for up to thirty miles in any direction."[1] This is almost unimaginable!

Who would ever know that something that seems so small and simple could be so huge! Jesus is just as huge as His name that was written across the sky on this day. The hymn, "The Love of God," so beautifully describes this scene exactly:

> *"Could we with ink the ocean fill*
> *And were the skies of parchment made*
> *Were every stalk on earth a quill*
> *And every man a scribe by trade*
> *To write the love of God above*
> *Would drain the ocean dry*
> *Nor could the scroll contain the whole*
> *Though stretched from sky to sky"*[2]

Isaiah 40:12 tells just how big God is. "Who hath measured the waters in the hollow of his hand, and meted out heaven with the span, and comprehended the dust of the earth in a measure, and weighed the mountains in scales, and the hills in a balance?" (KJV) You may be asking, "What are we to such a big God?" With a God this big, He must have an enormous love for us.

Ephesians 3:17-19 tells us, "That Christ may dwell in your hearts by faith; that ye, being rooted and grounded in love, May be able to comprehend with all saints what is the breadth, and length, and depth, and height; And to know the love of Christ, which passeth knowledge, that ye might be filled with all the fulness of God" (KJV). If God and his love are this huge, how insignificant are the problems we face? If He measured the waters in the hollow of His hand, can't He take care of us? Could it be that a simple act like a plane drawing lines in the sky could be a message from God?

That Christ may dwell in your hearts by faith; that ye, being rooted and grounded in love, May be able to comprehend with all saints what is the breadth, and length, and depth, and height; And to know the love of Christ, which passeth knowledge, that ye might be filled with all the fulness of God
Ephesians 3:17-19, KJV

OLD LOVE LETTERS

My husband Mark and I were cleaning out our closet when he handed me an old, romantic love letter that he wrote to me eleven years ago. Reading this letter reminded me how blessed I am to be loved by such a wonderful man and made me fall head-over-heels in love with him all over again. Of course, I have always been in love with him because he shows me his love every day through his kind words, hugs, compliments, helping around the house, and loving our daughter. 2 Corinthians 3:3 tells us that we can be letters from Christ, "written not with ink but with the Spirit of the living God, not on tablets of stone but on tablets of human hearts" (NIV). Jesus commanded that we love one another as He loved us.

My heart was full of love after reading Mark's love letter. To prove the fact that actions really *do* speak louder than words, I don't even remember reading this letter eleven years ago. I do remember the time that he helped me clean up after a sick baby in the wee hours of the night, knowing that he had to leave for work just three hours later. I also remember the time that he drove all the way across town to console my tender heart when I accidentally hit a dog on the way to work.

Be a letter from Christ by showing the depth of your love to others. Write the world a letter, written not with ink on tablets of paper, but on hearts. Words written in ink can fade away, but those written on hearts will be cherished always. You show that you are a letter from Christ, the result of our ministry, written not with ink but with the Spirit of the living God, not on tablets of stone but on tablets of human hearts.
2 Corinthians 3:3, NIV

HITTING BUTTERFLIES

I have a 75-mile per day commute to work that is quite challenging some days. I wake up and hurry to get dressed for work, make pancakes for my daughter, Krista, and an egg for my dog, Daisy. Yes, I make my dog an egg and not just any egg — she prefers hers scrambled with cheese. Krista is just like me — not a morning person. We are always rushing to school and rarely ever get there before the 8:00 bell rings, but somehow manage to arrive before the tardy bell. Our time management skills are surely lacking! After dropping Krista off at school, I rush to work. I try not to speed, but sometimes human nature takes over and I realize that I must wear some pretty heavy shoes.

On the way to work today, I noticed hundreds of little, yellow butterflies flying across the road — one or two at a time. They are so small that many people don't even notice them. God brought these little butterflies to my attention today, and I slowed down so I wouldn't hit them. I watched as the car in front of me sped right through them. Then I watched the gentle, yellow butterflies flap helplessly on the highway.

How many opportunities in life are we missing because we are so busy speeding through life that we don't even know what's going on? I find myself counting down the days of the week until Friday arrives. I even tell a co-worker, "Happy Friday Eve!" on Thursdays. How many people do we slow down to help? Instead of speeding through the week, perhaps we could help those people that God puts in our paths.

Another lesson I learned from the butterflies is the slower I go, the fewer butterflies I hit. The same could be said of our words. There would be less hurt in the world if we would speak less and listen more. Let us slow down and enjoy this ride we call life!

Wherefore, my beloved brethren, let every man be swift to hear, slow to speak, slow to wrath: For the wrath of man worketh not the righteousness of God.
James 1:19-20, KJV

LIVING WITH THE "JUNKYARD DOG"

I call my husband the "Junkyard Dog." He earns this title because he loves junkyards. He has always loved to work on cars, but that isn't the only reason he loves junkyards. In some of our most difficult financial times, we depended on those junkyards to make ends meet. My husband would research which parts were selling in online auctions, find the parts at the junkyard and sell the items for a large return. He once bought some side mirrors for $5 and started the auction at $9.99. Those mirrors sold for around $175! What seems like someone's wrecked piece of junk is my husband's treasure.

    I think of how God must love junkyards too. Not literally, but He does love to take people's wrecked lives and make them worth something. Like these old junk cars, we may think we have messed up our lives too much to be worth anything to such a Holy God, but the opposite is true. God loves our junk because through our junk, His glory shines through. Junkyards are also called "salvage yards." *The Free Dictionary* defines "salvage" as, "To save (discarded or damaged material) for further use."[3] What kind of testimony would a person have without a past? The quote, "God can turn our mess into a message" rings true.

Ephesians 2:4-5 says, "But God, who is rich in mercy, for his great love wherewith he loved us, Even when we were dead in sins, hath quickened us together with Christ, (by grace ye are saved;)..." (KJV). Although we were once just as dead in our sins as these rusty and wrecked cars, we are invaluable through salvation in Christ!

But God, who is rich in mercy, for his great love wherewith he loved us, Even when we were dead in sins, hath quickened us together with Christ, (by grace ye are saved;)...
Ephesians 2:4-5, KJV

MAIL FROM GRANDMA

> Hey Sugar Baby
> I saw this card & thought you'd like me to send it to you 'cause you like to get mail. I love you and am sending you a big Hug & Kiss thru Mama. Give Mama + dada a big hug & Kiss from me. We love you
> Granna & Poppa

My daughter Krista loves to go to the mailbox and find mail addressed to her. After moving to South Florida, Krista's grandma, whom she calls "Dannaw," began mailing little care packages to Krista as a way to keep in touch. Dannaw recently mailed Krista a pair of princess dress-up shoes that she purchased at the dollar store. After Krista wore the dress-up shoes for several days, they were broken, so Dannaw mailed a new pair. For the past two days, Krista has said, "Maybe I'll get some fancy shoes from Dannaw today," but the shoes haven't arrived yet. In reality, it costs more money to mail the packages than the gifts are actually worth, but they are priceless to Krista.

We are priceless to God. He paid the ultimate price of sending His son into the world as a baby and watching Him grow up to die. His redemption of our souls compares to Dannaw paying $5 to mail a $1 item. We will never be worthy of His great purchase, but we can dedicate our lives to Him and show how much we appreciate His great sacrifice.

Forasmuch as ye know that ye were not redeemed with corruptible things, as silver and gold, from your vain conversation received by tradition from your fathers; But with the precious blood of Christ, as of a lamb without blemish and without spot...
1 Peter 1:18-19, KJV

KEEPING WATCH

My friend Tammy and I took our kids to the park to enjoy the nice weather. As we were flying kites, we discovered two burrowing owls standing next to their nest in the ground. I have never seen an owl before, and was surprised to discover that not all owls are nocturnal. This particular owl dwells in burrows underground.

As I drew closer to take a picture, the female owl had walked back into the hole, but the male just watched me and screeched. The female owl reminded me of the story in the book of Matthew where the owner of the house didn't know the thief was coming and was neither prepared, nor keeping watch. The male owl reminded me of the Christian keeping watch for Christ's return. This owl was prepared, just as we should be. Christ is returning soon. Keep watch because we do not know what day He will come and we don't want to be unprepared.

"Therefore keep watch, because you do not know on what day your Lord will come. But understand this: If the owner of the house had known at what time of night the thief was coming, he would have kept watch and would not have let his house be broken into. So you also must be ready, because the Son of Man will come at an hour when you do not expect him..."

Matthew 24:42-44, NIV

TIGHT REIN

Have you ever had one of those moments when you just wanted to crawl under the nearest rock and hide? I had one of those moments today while we were walking our overweight dachshund around the neighborhood.

Daisy is a few pounds on the heavy side thanks to some fine dining in our household. We have been consistently walking Daisy around the neighborhood to help her lose some weight and stay active. As we were walking in the middle of the street, Daisy decided that it was a good place to do her business. How humiliating! Suddenly, a car flew around the corner and Krista jerked Daisy's leash to pull her to safety.

As Krista ran with the leash in hand, she realized that Daisy was not at the other end of the leash. Daisy remained squatted in the middle of the street. Her collar was so loose that it came off with the leash. I was afraid that the driver would hit Daisy, so I ran to her rescue. While we spent the next 30 minutes laughing hysterically over the incident, I realized how important it is to keep Daisy's collar tight. If the collar is too loose, it does no good! Daisy could become lost or injured without that collar. God gently nudged me and reminded me that the Bible also has something to say about keeping a tight rein.

Although it was definitely not a lesson that I wanted to hear, I have to pay attention when God is teaching — regardless of how hard it is to accept. James 1:26 says, "Those who consider themselves religious and yet do not keep a tight rein on their tongues deceive themselves, and their religion is worthless" (NIV).

James 1:19-20 also tells us exactly how to put a tight rein on our tongues. "My dear brothers and sisters, take note of this: Everyone should be quick to listen, slow to speak and slow to become angry, because human anger does not produce the righteousness that God desires" (NIV).

      Like Daisy's collar, if our words are loose, we can easily say something hurtful. Unfortunately, sticks and stones may break bones, but words really can hurt. When you say something that you don't mean, you can't take it back. I would hate to think that my Christian walk is worthless if I say something hurtful, but that's exactly what James 1:26 says. I'm going to tighten Daisy's collar now. I'll work on the tongue too!

Let the words of my mouth, and the meditation of my heart, be acceptable in thy sight, O Lord, my strength, and my redeemer.
Psalm 19:14, KJV

EARLY BIRDS

I love garage sale shopping, but don't go as often as I would like. A person can find all kinds of unique items at these sales and can tell much about the owners by the items they are selling. Some people shop at garage sales regularly, arriving early and waiting for the doors to open so that their treasures can be found. My friend Dana was having a garage sale a few years ago. As soon as she opened the garage door, she saw the feet of many customers who were anxiously waiting to find their treasures. Shopping early can really pay off!

Proverbs 8:17 says, "I love them that love me; and those that seek me early shall find me" (KJV). Many other versions of the Bible do not use the word "early" to describe how the Lord wants us to seek him, but the King James Version of this verse is beautiful to me. Just as those who are up at the break of dawn find their garage sale treasures, those who are this persistent in seeking God will find great treasure indeed.

I love them that love me; and those that seek me early shall find me. Riches and honour are with me; yea, durable riches and righteousness. My fruit is better than gold, yea, than fine gold; and my revenue than choice silver.
Proverbs 8:17-19, KJV

EMPTY DISH

This morning after breakfast, I discovered that my dog's water bowl was empty. As soon as I started filling her water dish with fresh water, she came running. I could tell that she was really thirsty for some fresh water. When her water bowl is dry, I will often find wet paw prints in the shower, where she has gone to lick water drops from the tub. If she would go to her water bowl and whine, I would know that her bowl is empty, but she doesn't know how to ask and is satisfied with simply licking drops of water from the bathroom tub.

Aren't we the same? Jesus has promised us living water, welling up. Instead of accepting this living water and enjoying fullness of life with Him, we often seek other things that will not fulfill us. Do we, like Daisy, not know how to ask for God to quench our thirsts, or are we simply satisfied with less than?

And the Spirit and the bride say, Come. And let him that heareth say, Come. And let him that is athirst come. And whosoever will, let him take the water of life freely.
Revelation 22:17, KJV

THE QUILT

Before Krista was born, my mother-in-law gave us a beautiful pink quilt that she made for our bed. It was lovely on our bed, but we also used it as a soft place for Krista to play and crawl when she was a baby. We watched her reach many developmental milestones on the comfort of this quilt. Some of the most beautiful quilts I've seen are called "crazy patchwork quilts." These quilts have no particular design, but use a variety of fabrics from different occasions or cultures — with each piece cut differently. The pieces of fabric are often stitched together with a variety of decorative stitches.

The church is similar to the quilt. We each have unique backgrounds, abilities, and personalities, but have a common interest as followers of Christ. When we come together as a group of believers, we are as magnificent as the crazy patchwork quilt. The church is there to provide comfort to those in need and to support those growing in the faith. Think of the church every time you see a beautiful quilt.

For just as each of us has one body with many members, and these members do not all have the same function, so in Christ we, who are many, form one body, and each member belongs to all the others.
Romans 12:4-5, NIV

THE LOST BEAD

My friend Tammy makes beautiful jewelry. Using ordinary beads, she makes very extraordinary jewelry. Just a few days ago, she made beautiful angel earrings out of four common beads. She told me how she was making a bracelet and accidentally dropped a bead on the floor. She diligently searched for the bead and was worried that she had lost it, but later found it right in front of her eyes. This would just be an ordinary bead to many people, but to Tammy, this bead was unique and would drastically change the appearance of the bracelet.

We are precious and irreplaceable to Jesus. Just as my friend rejoiced over finding the lost bead, all of heaven rejoices when we are found. Without this particular bead, other similar beads could not be a part of the bracelet because the sequence would be ruined. As we were once lost but now are found, we can also impact the lives of others and lead them to life as a beautiful creation in Christ.

"Or suppose a woman has ten silver coins and loses one. Doesn't she light a lamp, sweep the house and search carefully until she finds it? And when she finds it, she calls her friends and neighbors together and says, 'Rejoice with me; I have found my lost coin.' In the same way, I tell you, there is rejoicing in the presence of the angels of God over one sinner who repents."
Luke 15:8-10, NIV

THE EASTER CHICKS

My mom told me a story about some baby chicks that her parents brought home when she was little. At Easter time, baby chicks were sold in a variety of pastel colors. The children would "ooh" and "aah" over those precious colorful chicks and enjoy their pets for awhile, but soon the cuteness would wear off and the chicks became full-grown chickens.

My mom recalls a time when dinner was served and it was her beloved pets on the menu. Neither she, nor her siblings, would eat the chicken that was served that day. How could they possibly partake in something that was so precious to them?

I think about Jesus as a baby. God sent Him to Earth and He was just as precious and adorable as these cute little Easter chicks. I imagine how Mary felt when Jesus fluttered in her belly and how she felt when her little toddler took his first steps. All along, Mary and Joseph watched Jesus grow and reach new milestones.

God also watched His Son grow. He knew from the beginning what would happen, yet He made that costly sacrifice to send Jesus as a baby for sinners like us. God sent His precious baby Jesus for the thief who stole my bike this summer. He sent His Son for murderers, liars, and other sinners. Whether or not we want to admit it, we fit somewhere in there. Why would a Father make such a sacrifice like this? John 3:16 tells us, "For God so loved the world, that he gave his only begotten Son, that whosoever believeth in him should not perish, but have everlasting life" (KJV).

The really interesting part of this story — the chicks that my grandparents bought for their children were Easter chicks. These little colorful chicks were bought for the same holiday that is used to remember the sacrifice and Resurrection of Jesus. The next time you think of buying colorful chicks for your children, marshmallow chicks may be a better option.

For God so loved the world, that he gave his only begotten Son, that whosoever believeth in him should not perish, but have everlasting life.
John 3:16, KJV

CAKE BATTER

Krista and I love to bake cakes together. Her favorite part of baking is licking the batter from the bowl and spatula after the cake is in the oven. Sometimes waiting is difficult for Krista, and she doesn't want to wait for my help. One day while we were baking together, I turned my head to grab a utensil. Krista was attempting to pour a whole gallon of milk into the mixture without my help. She didn't want to wait, but the cake would have been a disaster without my help. Aren't we the same way with God?

In the Bible, Job suffered great loss and became angry and impatient with God. When Job repented and placed his trust in the all-knowing God, he was made prosperous and much was restored to him. We need to learn to wait on God and expect that things done in his will and timing will be perfect.

But the fruit of the Spirit is love, joy, peace, longsuffering, gentleness, goodness, faith, Meekness, temperance: against such there is no law.
Galatians 5:22-23, KJV

FLOWER PETALS

Last year I visited the supermarket to pick up a few items. Driving up in my dirty, pollen-covered van, I was immediately overwhelmed by the colors of spring. One tree in particular caught my attention. This tree had delicate, light pink flowers, and the wind had scattered some of the petals all over the parking lot. It reminded me of the petals a flower girl would drop down the aisle at a wedding. I praised God for such magnificent beauty and entered the store. When I returned to my van, I saw that it had been showered with hundreds of light pink flowers. I was amazed that God saw *my* old, dirty van worthy of being showered with these precious flowers, and I was reminded how unworthy I am to be loved by such a Savior.

Like the petals dropped by a flower girl at a wedding, my Creator saw me worthy of such splendor. I picked up a flower and gave it to Krista, showing her our love gift from the Lord. Jesus showers us with signs of His love daily. Could it be that every flower that your eye can see was made for your enjoyment, as well as His? When you praise Him for the work of His hands, He seems to display even more amazing things. Walk out in the yard and see all the flowers that God has put there for you to enjoy.

And why take ye thought for raiment? Consider the lilies of the field, how they grow; they toil not, neither do they spin: And yet I say unto you, That even Solomon in all his glory was not arrayed like one of these.
Matthew 6:28-29, KJV

RACCOON EYES

While on a mission trip, Krista and I took cold showers outside in a small tent area that accommodates approximately six people at a time. The tent and shower curtains are made from a tarp-like material, with clothes pins to hold the curtains together. As strange as it sounds, a cold shower is very refreshing after a hot day of street ministry. I quickly jumped in and out of the shower and returned to my room. If you are a woman who wears make-up, you know that mascara is difficult to remove and usually smears in the shower. Upon returning to my room, I told my two roommates that I must look like a raccoon because of the smeared mascara. At that exact moment, I looked up at the very top of the wall near the ceiling and saw a picture of two little raccoons. I started laughing out loud and knew deep down that God had a sense of humor and this was just His way of making me smile. I will never understand why the decorator hung the picture so high.

If you have ever hung a piece of art, you know that the rule of thumb is to hang the artwork at eye level, so that all the details can be seen and enjoyed. I doubt that many people have seen that raccoon picture at such a high level.

When people ask me about my writing, I am quick to tell them that all I do is pay close attention to what God puts before my eyes. Whatever sticks out in my mind in a given day is often an area that God is using to teach me something about Him and His attributes. God puts things out there for us to see, and we just have to pay attention long enough to see Him in all the details. Too often, our view of God is so far away that we can't see Him. We have to slow down in our daily activities and quiet ourselves to hear His gentle voice. When we do, He will reveal Himself to us in some ways that are truly amazing!

But as it is written, Eye hath not seen, nor ear heard, neither have entered into the heart of man, the things which God hath prepared for them that love him.
1 Corinthians 2:9, KJV

LITTLE BEGGAR

I was at home watching a cooking show with a chef making a delicious-looking pizza. I must admit that my mouth was watering for a slice, but Daisy really wanted a slice. When the chef held the freshly baked pizza for everyone to see, Daisy ran to the TV, threw her front paws into the begging position, and kindly begged for a slice of pizza. When Daisy begs for food, it is almost impossible to deny it to her. She begs with eager anticipation and sits as long as she can with her long, lean body trying to balance upright — wobbling from side to side. It seemed unrealistic for her to beg the chef on TV for some food, but it wasn't unrealistic for Daisy. Don't worry — I gave her plenty of good snacks later to make up for it. Through this, God reminded me that we need to have faith and persistence like Daisy.

In Luke, Jesus gives a parable about a widow who pleaded with a judge to grant her justice against her adversary. Back in that day, judges had their own agendas and would often not hear a case unless they were bribed. This widow would have had little money or influence because women were low on the social ladder. While many would have seen this as an impossible situation, the widow had faith and pleaded with the judge for justice. In Luke 18:7, we are told, "And shall not God avenge his own elect, which cry day and night unto him, though he bear long with them?" (KJV) If a judge who did not fear God or care about man was compelled by persistence to deal justly with a helpless widow, how much more will God answer our prayers? Like Daisy and this persistent widow, we must "come boldly unto the throne of grace, that we may obtain mercy, and find grace to help in time of need" (Hebrews 4:16, KJV).

Like Daisy's earthly master, our heavenly Master wants to bless us. Let us boldly approach the throne and expect our Master's blessing.

Now faith is the substance of things hoped for, the evidence of things not seen.
Hebrews 11:1, KJV

BIG BEN

For as long as I can remember, my mom has carried "Big Ben" around in her purse. Big Ben is a hundred dollar bill that she has carried around for years and refuses to ever spend, yet she will never leave home without it. As a child, I never understood why she would carry so much money, yet refuse to spend it. She explained that she would spend it if needed, but only in an emergency situation. What irony! My mom carries a valuable piece of money bearing the picture of a man who *had* been down to his last dollar.

PBS.org explains, "Franklin decided to become a vegetarian. He believed that eating a vegetarian diet was healthier than a diet filled with meat. In addition, meat was much more expensive, so by becoming a vegetarian, Franklin could save money to spend on books."[4] Franklin's autobiography tells how he bought three large rolls for a penny each. He ate one roll and gave the other two rolls to a woman with a child.[5]

Like Ben Franklin, the Apostle Paul knew what it was like to be in need. He wrote in Philippians 4:12-13, "I know what it is to be in need, and I know what it is to have plenty. I have learned the secret of being content in any and every situation, whether well fed or hungry, whether living in plenty or in want. I can do all this through him who gives me strength" (NIV).

Whether we are down to our last dollar, or we are carrying Big Ben in our purse or wallet, we can know that God is our true treasure.

But my God shall supply all your need according to his riches in glory by Christ Jesus.
Philippians 4:19, KJV

BUILDING ON THE SAND

My friend Tammy and I were discussing how we spent the weekend with our families. She told me about an air show that her family attended over the weekend. She described the stunts as being well-arranged and breathtaking. While she and her family attentively watched the show, one of her sons played in the sand — not interested in the events taking place. He was so engrossed in building a sand castle that he missed the main event.

Like this child, we can become so engrossed in the small things in life that we miss the most important part — our daily relationship with Christ. We can also miss spending time with those special people that He gave us to love. Let us build on what is solid, not on what will wash away with the tide.

And every one that heareth these sayings of mine, and doeth them not, shall be likened unto a foolish man, which built his house upon the sand: And the rain descended, and the floods came, and the winds blew, and beat upon that house; and it fell: and great was the fall of it.
Matthew 7:26-27, KJV

THE HARVEST MOON

Fall is just around the corner. Although the weather is still warm here, I see signs that indicate that fall is on its way. Last night I gazed upon an orange moon known as the Harvest Moon. The warm color drew me in and I thought about this moon all day. The Harvest Moon feels different to us because the moon is lower than usual in the fall season. The moon has a rich, orange color because when it is close to the horizon, it passes through more particles in the atmosphere, such as dirt and dust.

In historical times, extra light from the low position of the moon allowed farmers more time for harvesting. Is this a coincidence? No. Psalm 104:19 says, "He appointed the moon for seasons: the sun knoweth his going down" (KJV). The moon is closer to the horizon, so it looks and feels larger than it actually is.

I am amazed at how God takes into account every little detail of our lives, including something as simple as providing extra light to farmers in the harvest season. Harvesting had to be a big deal to these farmers — almost as big as this full moon.

We can relate to these farmers. The details in our lives seem like this bright, full moon — a big deal! Things that are close to us will naturally seem big or important. Whether there are big obstacles or big opportunities in our path, we are like this moon — just a speck in a huge universe. Still, God takes care of us just as He took care of the farmers. He cares so much about us that He even knows the number of hairs on our heads. With that kind of caring Father, whom or what should we fear?

When I consider thy heavens, the work of thy fingers, the moon and the stars, which thou hast ordained; What is

man, that thou art mindful of him? and the son of man, that thou visitest him?
Psalm 8:3-4, KJV

THE CANDLE

I recently attended a candle party that a friend hosted. I enjoy candles and burn them almost daily — savoring the different scents. As I anxiously await the arrival of my candle, I think of the delicious fragrance it will provide. As the flame melts the wax, the wax becomes very soft and shapeable. This is the perfect opportunity to reshape the candle back to its original design.

Like the candle, sometimes God uses fiery trials to soften our hearts and reshape them to be more like His. After God softens your heart, it can be formed to take on the shape of the heart of Christ.

A new heart also will I give you, and a new spirit will I put within you: and I will take away the stony heart out of your flesh, and I will give you an heart of flesh.
Ezekiel 36:26, KJV

PRAYING HANDS

My Uncle Leo was special to me. I always laughed when he said he was going to get his "beauty rest," meaning he was going to take his daily afternoon nap. I would joke and say, "You'd better sleep a long time then!" I specifically remember that he fell asleep with his hands together as if he were praying. It was only after he passed away that I discovered the real reason that he fell asleep this way. Uncle Leo suffered from a medical condition called "Essential Tremor" disorder, which caused his hands to shake. In order to fall asleep, he had to place his hands together to still them. How significant this is for us! When we fold our hands in prayer, we can be still and rest in a peace which passeth all understanding.

Be careful for nothing; but in every thing by prayer and supplication with thanksgiving let your requests be made known unto God. And the peace of God, which passeth all understanding, shall keep your hearts and minds through Christ Jesus.
Philippians 4:6-7, KJV

CRAB KILLER!

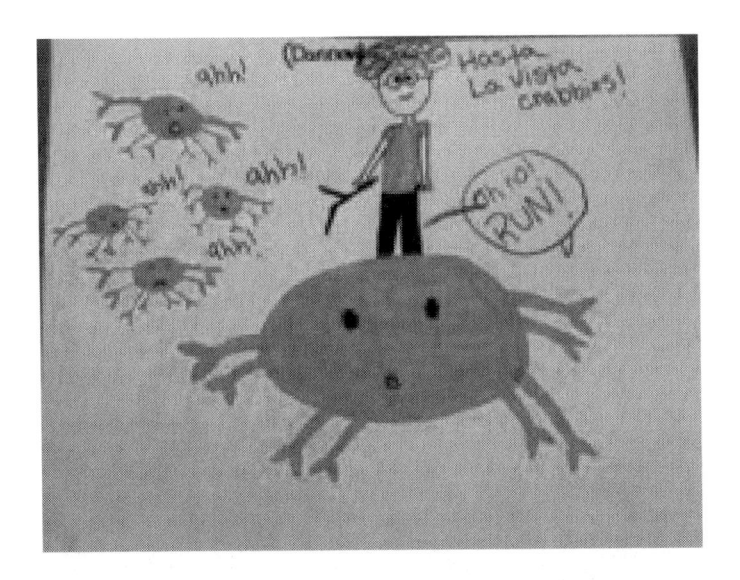

Krista and I went on a day trip with my parents to the beach. There is nothing better than watching your child build castles in the sand while listening to the waves rush in. The only thing that could be more entertaining is watching your 70-year old mother chase a fiddler crab with a small stick. It was a cute crab with eyes sticking out on top its head. My mom was only having fun with the crab, but it was ready to fight her before finally retreating into a hole to hide. Krista laughed as she watched her "Dannaw" chase the crab all over the beach that day. Krista knew that Dannaw had no intention of hurting the crab, but she still calls Dannaw the "Crab Killer" to this day. I often see myself as this little crab. At times, I feel like God is chasing me with a big stick. I let my mind get carried away with how He's going to punish me if I break one of His rules. The reality is that God does want my obedience, but He isn't there to hit me with a stick every time I fail. God is full of grace and love. The Bible tells us that nothing can separate us from the love of God — nothing! Just like the little crab, I can hide and try to separate myself from Him, but He will not remove His love from me.

For I know the thoughts that I think toward you, saith the LORD, thoughts of peace, and not of evil, to give you an expected end.
Jeremiah 29:11, KJV

DEAD BUG

Krista was examining a bug on the wall when it suddenly jumped on her. She screamed and I came to her rescue to kill the bug. Although the bug lay motionless on the floor, Krista insisted that it was still alive. My mom reminded me that I had the same fear when I was young, and she had to create a fake spider out of some black thread to make me believe that the spider was dead.

I believe that this is the child-like faith that we should exhibit to follow Jesus. We must know without a doubt that in spite of His death and burial, He was indeed resurrected and lives today. We can feel Him in our hearts even though we can't physically see Him. That is what faith is all about!

And as they were afraid, and bowed down their faces to the earth, they said unto them, Why seek ye the living among the dead? He is not here, but is risen: remember how he spake unto you when he was yet in Galilee, Saying, The Son of man must be delivered into the hands of sinful men, and be crucified, and the third day rise again.
Luke 24:5-7, KJV

COWBIRDS

When I was a child, we called egrets "cowbirds." Those little white cowbirds were always resting on top of cows or standing beside them. At such a young age, I never understood why the cows didn't just eat those pesky birds, or why the birds weren't afraid of the cows. I just assumed that it was a love/hate relationship and that the egrets loved the cows, while the cows tried to ignore the egrets. Now I realize that the cows probably appreciate the egrets because when the egret is there, the bugs and parasites aren't. The egrets feed on the bugs and parasites that would be harmful to the cows.

This is almost a perfect picture of abiding. Psalm 91:1 (KJV) says, "He that dwelleth in the secret place of the most High shall abide under the shadow of the Almighty." Verses 3-4 continue, "Surely he shall deliver thee from the snare of the fowler, and from the noisome pestilence. He shall cover thee with his feathers, and under his wings shalt thou trust: his truth shall be thy shield and buckler."

If that is not abiding, I don't know what is! God wants to abide with us, so why wouldn't we want to abide with him? He is power and life; in him there is no darkness. He is our comfort and our protection. Just as the cowbird is with the cow, God is there to help us. When we are troubled, He is a friend who will never leave us. Every time you see that little white bird, think of the Lord!

Surely he shall deliver thee from the snare of the fowler, and from the noisome pestilence. He shall cover thee with his feathers, and under his wings shalt thou trust: his truth shall be thy shield and buckler.
Psalm 91:1, 3-4, KJV

THE MYSTERIOUS MUSICIAN

I woke up at 3:30 AM, concerned that someone had broken into our home. Mark was sound asleep beside me, so I knew it wasn't him making the "ting-ting" sound that was coming from the other room. Should I wake him? Who could it be, and why is he playing my mandolin? What kind of person would break into our house in the middle of the night just to play an instrument? After realizing that this was a ridiculous assumption, I sought out the source of the music.

The music was coming from Krista's Celtic music CD that was playing in her bedroom, but I could only hear the higher pitches of the mandolin making a "ting-ting" sound. This reminded me of the verse in 1 Corinthians 13:1, "If I speak in the tongues of men or of angels, but have not love, I am only a resounding gong or a clanging cymbal" (NIV).

Much like the "ting-ting" sound of the mandolin, a cymbal can really add a lot to music, but who wants to hear only a cymbal played alone? Our drummer at church uses the cymbals on her drums to add dynamics to the music, but it would not sound like much if she only played the cymbals.

Just as the "ting-ting" sound is meaningless when played alone, we can do whatever we want in the name of Christ, but without love, it is only for ourselves. What is love? 1 John 4:8 tells us, "Whoever does not love does not know God, because God is love" (NIV). Do people see God in us, or do they only sporadically hear the "ting-ting" of our talk and actions? Do we do things for our own selfish gain, or do we truly love because we want to express God's love.

We love because he first loved us.
1 John 4:19, NIV

DAILY BREAD

Every summer "Big Boy" & "Happy Duck" return to the canal behind our home. Krista is always excited to see the ducks return, and she runs outside with bread to feed them. The ducks have healthy appetites, so we feed them twice a day. When the ducks see us from across the canal, they promptly swim over and run up the hill for their feeding. On extremely hot days, they rest under a shade tree in our backyard. As soon as the sliding glass door cracks, the ducks run to the door to beg for food. They have become very dependent on our provisions.

We can follow the example of Big Boy and Happy Duck and depend on God for our daily bread. Sometimes this bread is physical and sometimes it is spiritual. Jesus said in Luke 12:24, "Consider the ravens: for they neither sow nor reap; which neither have storehouse nor barn; and God feedeth them: how much more are ye better than the fowls?" (KJV)

> *Give us this day our daily bread.*
> Matthew 6:11, KJV

BABY POWDER

A few days ago, Krista and her friend were playing with their dolls. I watched as they fed their babies, changed their diapers, and put them to sleep. Since they were playing so well together, I decided to tend to chores in the other room. After a few minutes, I realized that it was too quiet and decided to check on them. The girls looked like two little ghosts, covered from head to toe in baby powder. I can laugh about it now, but it wasn't so funny when I had to clean up the mess.

Temptation is difficult for us all. Even Jesus was tempted by Satan for 40 days, but in His bodily weakness, He was able to reject Satan's attempts by quoting scripture. Satan cannot stand to hear the Word of God. When Jesus started quoting, Satan started running. Luke 4:13 says, "When the devil had finished all this tempting, he left him until an opportune time" (NIV). When we become tempted, we should use the example of Jesus and quote the Word of God. James 4:7 tells us, "Submit yourselves, then, to God. Resist the devil, and he will flee from you" (NIV).

There hath no temptation taken you but such as is common to man: but God is faithful, who will not suffer you to be tempted above that ye are able; but will with the temptation also make a way to escape, that ye may be able to bear it.
1 Corinthians 10:13, KJV

THE GRILL – UNDER CONSTRUCTION

I was driving to work when I saw a surprising sight. I had passed The Grill many times throughout my life and had eaten there before. What had been a well-known restaurant for many years was now being stripped and totally reconstructed into a new venue. I looked to see if there were any signs posted that might indicate what type of business would be at this location, but no information was provided. I could only wonder what type of restaurant or shop it may be. In months to come, I will surely know more.

Jeremiah 29:11 tells us, "For I know the plans I have for you," declares the LORD, "plans to prosper you and not to harm you, plans to give you hope and a future..." (NIV). Just as there were no signs to indicate what would become of the former grill, sometimes we go through major changes in our lives with no certainty of what the future may bring. We may not really like change, but it is certain in this life. No matter how your life is being reconstructed today, God can use it for His glory and for your good. Romans 8:28 tells us, "And we know that in all things God works for the good of those who love him, who have been called according to his purpose" (NIV).

Corrie Ten Boom so beautifully said, "Never be afraid to trust an unknown future to a known God."[6] These words that she spoke were not just empty words. Corrie ten Boom's home had literally gone through a reconstruction phase too! In the 1940s when the Nazis invaded the Netherlands, Corrie ten Boom's family renovated their home to include a secret room where refugees could hide. When the Nazis invaded their home in 1944, ten Boom and her family were arrested, but the

Jewish refugees who were hidden there were not discovered. When Corrie ten Boom was released she stated, "God does not have problems — only plans."[7]

Like the building under construction, we are presented with many changes and adjustments throughout life and don't always know the reason, or what the outcome will be. In months to come, what was formerly The Grill will be a new place of business. What is under construction in our lives will also come to fruition. In the process, will we see this construction as a problem or a divine plan?

"This is what the past is for! Every experience God gives us, every person He puts into our lives is the perfect preparation for a future that only He can see."[8]
~ Corrie ten Boom ~

CRUMB SNATCHER!

My dad told me a story about something that happened while he was working on a job one day. He has been in the painting and drywall business for many years. One day while taking his lunch break, he observed an army of ants that were working just as hard as he was. Displaying incredible strength, the ants carried a large crumb of food up the outer wall of the building. When the ants finally reached the top, a big cockroach ran out of nowhere and stole the large crumb, then ran out of sight. These poor ants probably felt that they had labored in vain. 2 Samuel 23:11-12 tells a story of one of David's mighty men, Shammah, son of Agee the Hararite. When the Philistines banded together at a place where there was a field full of lentils, Israel's troops fled from them. Shammah didn't flee, but stood firm in the middle of the field. He defended the field and struck the Philistines down, and the Lord brought about a great victory.

This can be a lesson for us all. When the devil sees that God is about to bless us, he wants to steal that blessing from us. John 10:10 says, "The thief cometh not, but for to steal, and to kill, and to destroy: I am come that they might have life, and that they might have it more abundantly" (KJV). Since the devil knows that we are children of God and that he can't take that away, he tries to discourage us with doubt or unbelief, frustration, and fear. Like Shammah, we need to stand up and defend our ground and watch the Lord bring about victory in our lives.

And let us not be weary in well doing: for in due season we shall reap, if we faint not.
Galatians 6:9, KJV

THE BUG

Krista is terrified of bugs. One rainy morning, I heard her screaming in her bedroom and ran to her rescue. She trembled with fear as she pointed to a bug on the floor. While I tried to kill the bug, Krista kept screaming and worrying. I just knew that her screaming would scare the bug away.

Isaac's wife must have also struggled with worry. Rebekah knew that her son, Jacob, should inherit the blessing of Isaac, but instead of praying and depending on God to accomplish what He promised, Rebekah decided to take matters into her own hands. She devised a plan that would result in many years of hardship for her son.

If we depend on God to take care of our problems, worry is unnecessary. We should present our requests to God in prayer, knowing that He is better equipped to handle our problems than we are. Our interference often harms rather than helps. We can fully submit control over to God and depend upon Him to carry our heavy loads.

Do not be anxious about anything, but in every situation, by prayer and petition, with thanksgiving, present your requests to God. And the peace of God, which transcends all understanding, will guard your hearts and your minds in Christ Jesus.
Philippians 4:6, NIV

NEW HEART

Some of God's most magnificent creatures live outside the screen of my back porch. A lizard can change colors to camouflage itself from harm and can even grow a new tail if its tail is torn. A lizard won't just give up if its tail is broken. Instead, it will grow a new tail.

Do you have a situation where your heart is torn in two? Just as God can give a lizard a new tail, He can also give you a new heart and a new spirit. He heals the brokenhearted and binds up their wounds.

A new heart also will I give you, and a new spirit will I put within you: and I will take away the stony heart out of your flesh, and I will give you an heart of flesh.
Ezekiel 36:26, KJV

THE BLOOD DONATION BUS

While driving one Sunday, we passed a large church. The lot was full of cars, and a blood donation bus was parked in front to receive blood donations. I had never seen a blood donation bus at a church before. *How strange*, I thought, *yet how ironic*. Watching people enter and exit the blood donation bus reminded me of biblical times when people went to the temple for the priests to make sacrifices with the shed blood of animals for the forgiveness of sins.

I'm certain that the recipients of the blood donations were grateful for the donations given at this church. According to the Mayo Clinic, "Each whole blood donation may help as many as three people...On average, a hip replacement typically uses one unit of blood, a cardiac bypass two units, a heart transplant two units, and a liver transplant six units."[9] One donor can make a huge difference, but sometimes even one donor isn't enough to save a life!

Many people who donate blood are so fulfilled by giving that they continue to give blood as often as possible. According to *USA Today*, the man who held the world record for the most whole blood donations donated 315 pints.[10] He still doesn't hold the highest record, however.

A man who walked among us nearly 2,000 years ago saved countless lives, and here's the amazing part – it was only through one donation of shedding His blood on the cross. What men have had to do for years through sacrifice, Jesus did once and for all on the cross. *"What can wash away my sin? Nothing but the blood of Jesus!"*[11]

Neither by the blood of goats and calves, but by his own blood he entered in once into the holy place, having obtained eternal redemption for us.
Hebrews 9:12, KJV

THE TASTY PINK PURSE!

I am not a regular entertainer, but we occasionally have people over. When we have visitors, my dog goes bananas! Daisy is the friendly greeter in our household, but sometimes she is a bit too friendly! Some friends met at our house last night for fellowship, and Daisy was being her usual overly-friendly self. Everyone seemed "ok" with Daisy except Carla, who would gently shoo Daisy away with her foot. You have to understand Carla. She is a very attractive lady who dresses stylish — with matching shoes and purse. Carla is just not an animal lover, and we all find it humorous to see how pets drive her crazy. What I may never tell her is that after shooing Daisy away several times, Carla turned her head in conversation, and Daisy started licking her cute, pink purse — and I mean really licking it! I moved Daisy away from the purse, but Carla would die if she knew. This may be a secret that I have to take to my grave, but just because Carla didn't see it doesn't mean it didn't happen. Carla didn't see it, but I did!

God sees all the things we do too — both good and bad. He is known as Jehovah El Roi, the God who sees. He saw Hagar when she thought she was invisible. He saw Nathaniel under the fig tree. He even saw Adam and Eve when they sinned in the garden. He also sees our needs, struggles, victories, and all the good or bad things we do. He even saw Daisy lick Mrs. Carla's purse and guilty Amy not tell her about it.

Your friends may not see your hurt, your boss may not see your hard work, and your family may not see how much you've sacrificed for them, but GOD sees all!

The eyes of the LORD are in every place, beholding the evil and the good.
Proverbs 15:3, KJV

"INSONGNIA"

When my cousin Andrea was twelve, she invented the word "insongnia" to describe having a song stuck in your mind. This is the most frustrating experience because the song repeats over and over like a broken record — often lasting for several hours or even days. Today I have a song stuck in my head that I wish I could expel. The only way to remove a song from your head is to listen to a new song and replace the old song.

In the book of Psalms, David makes several references to putting a new song in his mouth. I can just imagine David tending to his sheep at night and admiring the beauty of God's creation — the moon and the stars. He starts humming a song, pulls out his flute to play, and lifts his voice in praise to his Creator. When I was a child, my dad often took his banjo to the backyard where he would play music and sing songs of worship. This is how I imagine that David praised God. David was not perfect and made several mistakes because even children of God sin. Despite his faults, he loved God and repented of his sins. Through David's repentance, God replaced the broken record of sin with a new song of forgiveness, love, and praise.

And he hath put a new song in my mouth, even praise unto our God: many shall see it, and fear, and shall trust in the LORD.
Psalm 40:3, KJV

THE PINE TREE CROSS

I sometimes become anxious over the smallest things. One day, Mark had an interview for what I thought would be the perfect job. My anxiety escalated, and I immediately prayed for peace for us both — whether or not he got the job. As I waited for him to return from the interview, something caught my eye. I discovered a pine tree cross lying on the ground, and an amazing peace covered me like a blanket.

You will notice that just before Easter, some pine trees form shoots in the shape of a cross. While some scientific explanation probably exists, I personally believe that God's creation is giving Him glory at this special time of year. God allowed me to find this cross in the yard to remind me that even when we suffer disappointments here, His death on the cross ensures the ultimate victory. Nothing can compare to what eternity holds for us.

Do not be anxious about anything, but in every situation, by prayer and petition, with thanksgiving, present your requests to God. And the peace of God, which transcends all understanding, will guard your hearts and your minds in Christ Jesus.
Philippians 4:6-7, NIV

MRS. WREN

With spring approaching, my aunt awaits the arrival of "Mrs. Wren," an extremely persistent bird that lived in her carport last year. Without fail, every time Aunt Evelyn would open the door to go outside, Mrs. Wren would try to fly in the door to prepare a nest for her new baby birds. She would even hide in the hedges and wait for the perfect opportunity to enter. It was as though my aunt's back porch was her own little vision of Heaven.

While Mrs. Wren was a nuisance to my aunt, she was an example to me. Just as Mrs. Wren was waiting for the perfect opportunity to fly in, we should be alert and ready. Instead, we become distracted by the busyness of life and take our focus off what is most important. Meaningless tasks take priority over our quiet times. We often miss spending quality time with those we love and neglect to tell others about Christ. Just as Mrs. Wren had her eyes focused on her main purpose, we should focus on our purpose and be ready for every opportunity.

Looking unto Jesus the author and finisher of our faith; who for the joy that was set before him endured the cross, despising the shame, and is set down at the right hand of the throne of God.
Hebrews 12:2, KJV

DADDY'S LITTLE HELPER

I watched as Krista helped her daddy work on his car. While he was making repairs to the car, she sat on his back and handed him every tool she could find. She was so proud to have helped Daddy fix the car.

Are we this eager to help the people around us? Who can you help today? Perhaps there is a single parent who needs a babysitter so that she can have some time to herself, or a friend who needs someone to listen. I remember when an elderly lady approached me at the gas pump one day. She explained that she didn't know how to pump gas because her husband always kept her tank filled, but he was in the hospital and she didn't know what to do. These are the people who need us the most.

Helping others fills us with joy because we have not only helped someone in need, but we have also served the Lord.

"The King will reply, 'Truly I tell you, whatever you did for one of the least of these brothers and sisters of mine, you did for me.'"
Matthew 25:40, NIV

GRAPES OF FAITH

Upon leaving South Florida, we were faced with difficulties at every angle. I had been sick and was prepared for the upcoming hurricane, but was not prepared with the types of food that my sickness required. Mark would be starting a new job the following week, and we had not finished packing for the move. Without power for nearly a week, we were unable to contact the rental truck company. I knew that this move was God's will for us because He had already revealed that, but with so many problems arising, I questioned our decision. Later that day, my neighbor brought us some grapes, French bread, a diet soft drink, and water. She didn't realize that she was on a mission from God.

The Israelites who followed Moses seemed very stubborn. How many times would God have to prove his faithfulness and supernatural ability before they would finally believe? My trial at that time proved that I am no different. Although God has proven faithful to me numerous times, a new crisis brings new doubts.

In Numbers 13, Moses sent spies out to explore the land of Canaan. They returned with such an extraordinary cluster of grapes that it had to be carried on a pole between two men. This was no ordinary cluster of grapes, but the first ripe grapes from the first harvest when the grapes looked and tasted their best. Although the cluster of grapes was enormous, the Bible indicates that the spies only brought back one cluster. This reaffirms God's ability to turn something small and ordinary into something extraordinary. Still, the Israelites doubted and planned to return to Egypt. In Numbers 14:9, Joshua & Caleb compared the people of Canaan to bread. This bread would be easily broken and defeated and would provide them with the strength they needed to persevere.

My neighbor in South Florida did not realize our struggles when she provided us with the grapes and bread. Matthew 7:20 tells us that you will recognize a tree by the fruit it bears. My neighbor was bearing fruit in the likeness of Christ. Like the spies, my neighbor came bearing a cluster of grapes that would remind us that God was blessing us in this new transition and he had great plans for us. I don't know whether my neighbor only had a single cluster like the spies, but she shared her first fruits — her most precious grapes, in a time of need. She also brought a loaf of bread like the bread that Joshua and Caleb compared the people of Canaan to. I would later realize that through this gift of bread, God was communicating that we would overcome the trial we faced and that this trial would give us strength to persevere when we struggled in faith again. Who would think that a single act of kindness was a meeting arranged by God?

Even so every good tree bringeth forth good fruit; but a corrupt tree bringeth forth evil fruit. A good tree cannot bring forth evil fruit, neither can a corrupt tree bring forth good fruit. Every tree that bringeth not forth good fruit is hewn down, and cast into the fire. Wherefore by their fruits ye shall know them.
Matthew 7:17-20, KJV

THE CREPE MYRTLE

A few weeks ago, Mark and my father-in-law decided to prune our Crape Myrtle tree. This tree towered high above the house before they decided to cut it. Watching them prune the tree was painful. I asked them to stop cutting the tree because it looked terrible. My father-in-law said that although it seemed drastic, pruning the tree would increase the blooms. With summer approaching, I wait anxiously to see the new growth.

The Bible tells us that God prunes us to rid us of fruitless branches. We may end up losing things or people that we would rather not lose. It may be a job, an activity we enjoy, or even a friend. Although it is painful to lose these branches, God knows what is essential for better growth.

I remember a painful time when Mark was laid off from a job. Right before he lost the job, things had been stressful at work. I came in one day to find him digging through a cardboard box full of personal items from his desk. Not knowing how we would make it through the next few months felt like a fresh cut, but through this experience, God showed us that He is our provision and help in times of trouble. The next job proved God's sovereignty. Although Mark took a huge cut in pay, the benefits were great and his new job was less stressful. Like the fresh growth on the tree, we had a new trust in God.

"I am the true vine, and my Father is the gardener. He cuts off every branch in me that bears no fruit, while every branch that does bear fruit he prunes so that it will be even more fruitful..."
John 15:1-2, NIV

CALLUSES

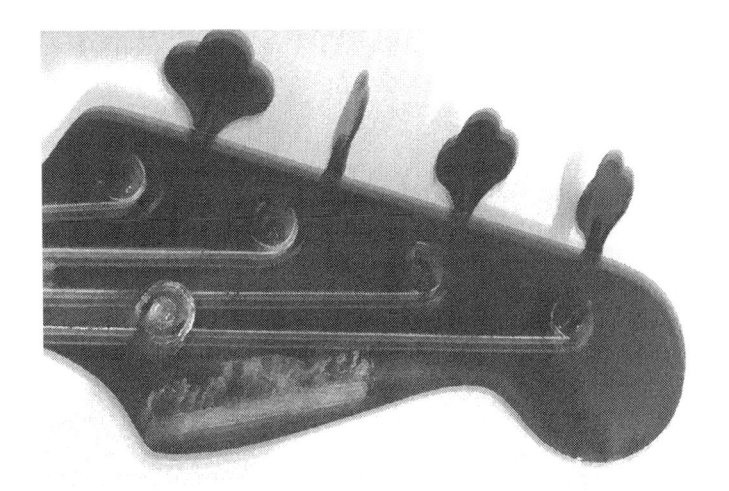

They are a musician's best friend, but cannot be bought for any price. They are a hand model's worst enemy, and she may even pay to have them removed. Just last week, a co-worker was telling me that she went to the doctor to have calluses removed from her hands, yet many musicians would pay top dollar to have calluses on their fingers. Playing a stringed instrument takes time, practice, and pain! Fingers are naturally tender, and the repetitive plucking or sliding of the fingers on a stringed instrument can leave fingers tender and blistered. I have played many times until blisters formed, and I had to wait until the pain ceased and blisters diminished before playing again. After playing for several weeks, the soft, blistered skin is replaced with tough skin called calluses. The calluses help the musician's fingers slide more easily, and the musician can play for longer periods of time without pain. Even with calluses, tenderness can occur if a musician plays for long periods of time, but the calluses definitely help protect the fingers.

My brother Les told me the importance of keeping in practice and warned, "If you lose your calluses, you won't be able to play." It was true! After not playing for several months, my fingers became soft and tender and wouldn't glide across the strings. It was painful all over again.

Like a musician's fingers, we all go through painful times in life. Sometimes our pain can last for months or years. James 1:2-4 says, "Consider it pure joy, my brothers and sisters, whenever you face trials of many kinds, because you know that the testing of your faith produces perseverance. Let perseverance finish its work so that you may be mature and complete, not lacking anything" (NIV).

A musician knows that his pain will lead to calluses, which will make him stronger and more efficient. We can also know that our pain in life will make us stronger and more mature in the end. We will be able to look back and see the fiery trials that we've endured and know that God not only brought us through them, but that He is fully able to handle all of our trials to come.

I can do all this through him who gives me strength.
Philippians 4:13, NIV

BUNDLE OF FLOWERS

When Krista was a toddler, I remember taking her shopping with me one day and watching her have a meltdown over a bundle of artificial flowers that she did not need. We've all been there when a child starts screaming in public. The mother does everything to control the child, but the child screams relentlessly. We simply turn around and mumble, "If that were my child...." This time it *was* my child! Krista screamed so loudly that people on the other side of the store turned around to look at her. She was overly tired that day because she missed her nap, but the fact that it wasn't her usual behavior didn't change the outcome.

I think of how our Heavenly Father must feel about our behavior at times. I've had my own share of negative encounters with people and was embarrassed afterwards by my own behavior. From road rage to getting aggravated with rude store clerks, I have not always acted as I should. Before we act, we should consider how our behavior may seem to those around us. Would our behavior resemble that of a Christ-follower?

For the grace of God that bringeth salvation hath appeared to all men, Teaching us that, denying ungodliness and worldly lusts, we should live soberly, righteously, and godly, in this present world; Looking for that blessed hope, and the glorious appearing of the great God and our Saviour Jesus Christ; Who gave himself for us, that he might redeem us from all iniquity, and purify unto himself a peculiar people, zealous of good works.
Titus 2:11-14, KJV

FIREFLIES

I remember watching fireflies light up the sky when I was young and trying to figure out the reason for their fascinating ability. We recently moved into a new house, and I am anxious to see if fireflies will illuminate our yard in the summer. For years, children have caught fireflies to watch them glow and try to reveal the mystery behind their remarkable ability. *Scientific American* gives a description of this phenomenon called bioluminescence. "When oxygen combines with calcium, adenosine triphosphate (ATP) and the chemical luciferin in the presence of luciferase, a bioluminescent enzyme, light is produced."[12] *Wikidot* also explains, "All phenomena of bioluminescence rely on a relatively simple reaction between a biomolecule and an enzyme, called luciferin and luciferase, respectively. (These names come from the Latin 'lucifer,' meaning 'light-bearer')."[13] If this sounds familiar, the Bible makes reference to Lucifer when it says, "And no marvel; for Satan himself is transformed into an angel of light" (2 Corinthians 14:11, KJV).

While fireflies are beautiful and use flashes of light to communicate and defend themselves, there are some predator fireflies that are out for an attack. One such species has learned to mimic the flash of other species. *Kemana Perginya Kelip-Kelip* explains, "Some types of adult fireflies are predators. And some predatory females have learned a way to an easy meal. They have learned the flashing patterns of other species. They flash a male of another species and when he lands to mate, she kills him and eats him."[14]

As Christians, we must beware of such predators. It is when we are illuminated by Christ and serving as a light to the dark world that the fallen angels attack. We have all been around Satan's campfire before we were guided by the light of Christ. For this reason, Satan knows our weaknesses and will use them against us. He has seen our reactions and knows exactly what would cause us to fall. Like the predator firefly, he seeks to devour us and put out our light to the world.

As Peter said in 1 Peter 5:8-9, "Be sober, be vigilant; because your adversary the devil, as a roaring lion, walketh about, seeking whom he may devour: Whom resist stedfast in the faith, knowing that the same afflictions are accomplished in your brethren that are in the world" (KJV). The devil will attempt to put out our lights, but it is written in Isaiah 30:21, "And thine ears shall hear a word behind thee, saying, This is the way, walk ye in it, when ye turn to the right hand, and when ye turn to the left" (KJV).

For ye were sometimes darkness, but now are ye light in the Lord: walk as children of light: (For the fruit of the Spirit is in all goodness and righteousness and truth;) Proving what is acceptable unto the Lord. And have no fellowship with the unfruitful works of darkness, but rather reprove them.
Ephesians 5:8-11, KJV

GRILLING STEAKS

A few years ago, a friend and I decided to surprise our husbands by grilling steaks for dinner. The only problem was that neither of us knew how to use a charcoal grill. To make a long story short, we had flames of fire nearly touching the roof of the outdoor patio, and we almost had to call for help. Because we had no one to counsel us on grilling techniques, our plans failed, and our expensive steaks were ruined.

Proverbs 15:22 tells us that our plans fail for lack of counsel. In our daily walk, we have someone who is willing to help us and will counsel us as to which way to go. We can always seek counsel from our Wonderful Counselor — our Mighty God.

For unto us a child is born, unto us a son is given: and the government shall be upon his shoulder: and his name shall be called Wonderful, Counsellor, The mighty God, The everlasting Father, The Prince of Peace.
Isaiah 9:6, KJV

THE HARMONICA

Every Christmas Eve my dad and I, along with some friends, like to take our instruments to the local hardware store, where we play Christmas carols for the employees and customers. It is our own way to spread Christmas cheer to the community. Krista decided to come with us this year, but she was disappointed that although she had learned to play some Christmas carols on the saxophone, she left her instrument at home — an hour away. My dad told her, "Krista, you should always come prepared with something to play — wherever you go." He pulled a harmonica out of his shirt pocket and showed it to her, telling her that he never leaves home without it. I knew very well that this was true. I specifically remember going with him on a trip to the mountains one time when he forgot his harmonica. We had to stop on the way to buy one just so he would have something to play in the car, or for whomever he saw along the way.

Just as my dad is always prepared with his harmonica, the Bible tells us to be prepared. "But sanctify the Lord God in your hearts: and be ready always to give an answer to every man that asketh you a reason of the hope that is in you with meekness and fear..." (1 Peter 3:15, KJV). We never know when someone is going to ask the reason for our hope or faith. We should always be prepared to give our testimony and the reason for our hope. We might also have some Bible verses memorized too, so that we can help a brother or sister along the way.

I love the LORD, because he hath heard my voice and my supplications. Because he hath inclined his ear unto me, therefore will I call upon him as long as I live.
(Psalm 116:1-2, KJV)

REDHEAD

I had an appointment with my hairdresser today and have a bold new look — perhaps a little too bold! I have had blonde highlights all of my adult life, but now have dark red hair. I'm wondering if I should wear a scarf or a hat to work tomorrow because I'm concerned about what people will think of the new color. After my hair appointment, I came home and washed my hair twice to tame down the red color, but no matter how much I wash, the dye is permanent and here to stay.

This experience made me think about my salvation. Isaiah 1:18 says, "though your sins be as scarlet, they shall be as white as snow; though they be red like crimson, they shall be as wool" (KJV). You see, if I want to get rid of the red color in my hair, I can't just wash the color away because permanent color is just that — *permanent*! Instead, my hairdresser will have to fix it. Sin is exactly the same. We cannot get rid of our sin by anything we do. Jesus is the Lamb of God, and takes away the sin of the world. Only He can wash the sin away.

For I am persuaded, that neither death, nor life, nor angels, nor principalities, nor powers, nor things present, nor things to come, Nor height, nor depth, nor any other creature, shall be able to separate us from the love of God, which is in Christ Jesus our Lord.
Romans 8:38-39, KJV

FORSAKEN!

Krista and I spent last Saturday with our cousin Ashley. Krista loves spending time with Ashley, just as I always loved spending time with my cousins. When I was a child, I spent many weekends with my cousins, Lisa, Betty Sue, Robin, and Roger. Krista loves spending time with her cousins too!

We made plans to do many fun things with Ashley, including a costume 5K fun run. We all dressed in cat costumes and made our way to the event. We weren't exactly prepared to run a 5K, so we lagged behind in the race with only a lone elderly gentleman behind us. As we dragged ourselves up a dark, steep hill, the older gentleman made us a solemn promise. "You girls stay ahead of me and I won't let you come in last place." That was reassuring to us because the thought of an elderly man beating three younger ladies was a little humiliating.

As we neared the end of the loop, we realized that our elderly friend had not kept his promise. Instead, he passed us and left us in the dust. So much for promises!

When Moses was 120 years old, he made a similar promise to the people of Israel. He knew he wouldn't be able to cross Jordan, but he gave a solemn promise — that the LORD God would never leave them nor forsake them. "Be strong and courageous. Do not be afraid or terrified because of them, for the LORD your God goes with you; he will never leave you nor forsake you" (Deuteronomy 31:6, NIV).

At times, we don't feel we can trust others to keep their promises. The Bible says that some may even be forsaken by their own family. Psalm 27:10 tells us, "When my father and my mother forsake me, then the LORD will take me up" (KJV).

I have a friend who once told me that it was hard to know the love of the Heavenly Father because she never knew the love of her earthly father. Psalm 68:5-6 tells us that God is, "A father to the fatherless, and a judge of the widows...God setteth the solitary in families: he bringeth out those which are bound with chains..." (KJV).

Whether you feel forsaken by a family member, have lost a loved one in death, or have been betrayed by a friend or co-worker, you can be sure that God is a Father who will never forsake us. He will be there at every step of our journey in life!

Teaching them to observe all things whatsoever I have commanded you: and, lo, I am with you always, even unto the end of the world. Amen.
Matthew 28:20, KJV

HAPPY DUCK

Happy the Duck frequently swims in the canal behind our house and camps out in our backyard most of the summer. On my way home from the grocery store, I saw Happy crossing a busy street near our house. After taking a step into the street, the duck saw an oncoming car and froze for several seconds. As the car slammed on brakes, Happy waddled as fast as she could across the street. During the few seconds that she paused, I'm sure Happy was thinking that she was a dead duck!

Peter probably felt the same way when he walked on the water toward Jesus. As he doubted and began to sink, Jesus reached out and caught him, asking, "O thou of little faith, wherefore didst thou doubt?" (Matthew 14:31, KJV) How deep is your faith? Can you rely on God to be your lifeguard? If God made the winds, He is surely able to calm them.

And immediately Jesus stretched forth his hand, and caught him, and said unto him, O thou of little faith, wherefore didst thou doubt?
Matthew 14:31, KJV

LOST TRACKS

Before we bought our home, we knew that a train ran somewhere behind the house because we saw the tracks on the city map. After moving in, Mark searched the woods behind our house for the train tracks, but couldn't locate them. There were, indeed, train tracks behind our house, but because they were lying diagonal to our house, he couldn't find them. When the train comes by, we can see its bright light flashing through the trees from the west into the east and hear the thunder echo through the lonely woods. Of course, we are so used to hearing the train that we occasionally tune out the sound when the train comes barreling by. It's a sound we really enjoy and is a constant reminder of God's presence.

Sometimes the pressures of life can be difficult, and in our searching and wandering, we question where God is. Like the train tracks, sometimes we don't know that God is there because we don't know how to seek Him or listen for His voice. Jesus is like the light on the train, shining His light.

When the wise men saw the bright star shining in the east, they knew that it had to be of God and that something magnificent had taken place. Although they had no solid proof of the little Savior's birth, the wise men followed the star without hesitation. When we are in need of the presence of God, He only asks that we seek Him with all of our heart. Then we will see His light flashing into our dark and lonely world. He may offer this light by a scripture we read, a sermon we hear, a Christian friend's counsel, or a deep feeling of peace. Once you find God, you will never want to be out of His presence again!

And thou, Solomon my son, know thou the God of thy father, and serve him with a perfect heart and with a willing mind: for the LORD searcheth all hearts, and understandeth all the imaginations of the thoughts: if thou seek him, he will be found of thee; but if thou forsake him, he will cast thee off for ever.
1 Chronicles 28:9, KJV

THE UNEXPECTED VISITOR

I recently attended a funeral of a family member who passed away. To my surprise, when the service began, our deceased loved one's large dog marched down the church aisle and up to the casket to see his master one last time. I was shocked that someone would bring a dog to a church service, but especially to a funeral. The more I thought about it, the more I realized that this dog was like a special family member to his master, just as the rest of the family was.

God reminded me of times when I was judgmental of other people, just as I was judgmental of the dog attending the funeral. Although Jesus shed the same blood on the cross for those people as He shed for me, sometimes I tend to be judgmental of them. In reality, God loves them just as much as He loves me. If God loves them this much, then I should too. I guess a dog really can be man's best friend!

A new commandment I give unto you, That ye love one another; as I have loved you, that ye also love one another. By this shall all men know that ye are my disciples, if ye have love one to another.
John 13:34-35, KJV

THE CURTAIN

Today was supposed to be observation day at Krista's ballet class. Mark came with me to watch the rehearsal, but we were disappointed when the instructor closed the curtains and announced that observation day had been delayed so that the children could learn new dance techniques. We were only able to wait outside the curtain and listen to the dancing and music, while trying to imagine what the children were learning to do.

As a child of God, I often ask why things happen as they do. Why do innocent babies die? Why are people starving throughout the world? Why do those who do evil prosper, while those who do good suffer? As we come to the end of our journey on Earth and the curtain is opened, all the mysteries will be revealed.

For my thoughts are not your thoughts, neither are your ways my ways, saith the LORD. For as the heavens are higher than the earth, so are my ways higher than your ways, and my thoughts than your thoughts.
Isaiah 55:8-9, KJV

JUST ONE STRIKE!

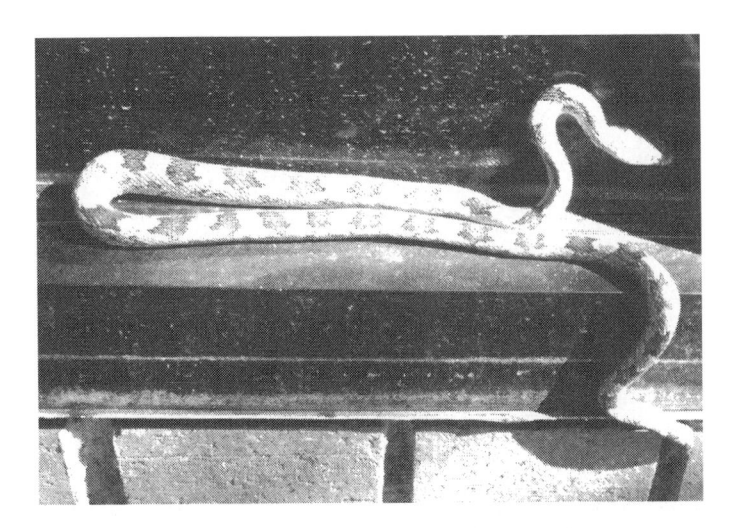

I am not an outdoor girl! I don't enjoy getting dirt under my nails or mud on my clothes, but my yard was overgrown with weeds, and I figured I'd better clean out some of the weeds because it was looking like the perfect home for a snake. Out the door I went with a hoe in one hand and a metal rake in the other. I stayed a few feet away from the area I raked in case there was a snake hiding underneath the pine straw. Alas, a snake appeared! It was only a small snake, but a snake is a snake! I grabbed the hoe and chopped away at the snake yelling, "Take that!" I was quite proud that I had destroyed the snake, and I watched his body wriggle back and forth. Wait a minute — it was only a tail! Then I watched as the rest of the snake's body disappeared into the moist ground. This wriggling reaction was caused by nerves in the snake's body, but also serves as a defense mechanism for escaping enemies. In my own strength, I tried to kill the snake, but because I didn't strike its head, the snake was undefeated.

The Bible says in Luke 10:19, "Behold, I give unto you power to tread on serpents and scorpions, and over all the power of the enemy: and nothing shall by any means hurt you" (KJV). This verse explains that it is by God's power that we can defeat the enemy — not our own power. In 1 Samuel 26:8, I believe that Abishai understood the great power of God. Speaking of Saul, who was out to take David's life, Abishai said, "God hath delivered thine enemy into thine hand this day: now therefore let me smite him, I pray thee, with the spear even to the earth at once, and I will not smite him the second time" (KJV).

With the power of God, we are able to overcome all that the enemy throws at us. Just as I became distracted by the snake's wiggling tail, let us not become distracted by all the trials that Satan throws our way. Instead, have faith like Abishai. With God's power flowing through us and authority in Jesus' name, we have the power to defeat the enemy with just one strike.

Behold, I give unto you power to tread on serpents and scorpions, and over all the power of the enemy: and nothing shall by any means hurt you.
Luke 10:19, KJV

ONE MAN'S TRASH

One of my greatest treasures was found in my neighbor's trash. A few years ago, the Lord asked me to do something that was hard for me to do, but I knew it was something I should do. As soon as I got in my car and said, "Lord, I surrender and will do this for you," I backed out of my driveway and discovered a beautiful painting in my neighbor's trash. The painting was in magnificent condition — complete with a frame.

This oil painting depicted Jesus as a toddler, taking some of his first steps. As he ran with his arms outstretched, the perfect shadow of a cross was cast behind him. He was walking toward the door, which led to a cross on a distant mountain outside. It was as though the painting was giving a glimpse of Jesus' future. This painting taught me about sacrifice. My sacrificial offering that day was very small compared to that which Jesus faced. I would not trade this painting for anything in the world because I consider it my love gift from God. Sometimes God gives us love gifts here, as well as in heaven.

Rejoice ye in that day, and leap for joy: for, behold, your reward is great in heaven: for in the like manner did their fathers unto the prophets.
Luke 6:23, KJV

IN PERFECT HARMONY

I grew up in a family that traveled to various churches to play bluegrass gospel music. When my dad told us to stick with him and he'd take us places, he wasn't kidding! One place he took us to was to a little church in Alabama where we were treated to bologna sandwiches for dinner. The sandwiches sat on the table of the fellowship hall for so long that the thick mayonnaise had turned clear!

Playing music in these little churches brings back great memories. We always had some of the most memorable experiences in the most unexpected places. I also learned about life through music. A person singing harmony may sound off key if she is singing alone, but when she sings with a lead vocal and another harmony vocal, it is a very fine combination. Our lives are this way too. Without the Trinity, (God, Jesus, and the Holy Spirit) we are not in perfect harmony. We can't have God without believing in salvation through Jesus, and we need the Holy Spirit for guidance and comfort. These three make a perfect combination.

Serve the LORD with gladness: come before his presence with singing.
Psalm 100:2, KJV

A LITTLE "WARM-UP"

My friend Michelle and I share a coffee pot at work. Just the other day, Michelle came into my office with only a little coffee in her cup and said, "Let me get a little more coffee to warm this up." I have heard my dad say this many times before, so when Michelle asked, it brought back sweet memories. I always get more coffee to drink, but never thought of it as warming up what I already have. Some people only like their food and drink hot. I have a friend who will send his food back at a restaurant if it isn't piping hot when it is brought out. I was more than happy to give Michelle a "warm-up" of coffee. I then realized that my own life needs a "warm-up" at times too.

Sometimes I feel spiritually and emotionally empty — like I'm not feeling God is there, or I am a little down. Like my friend who has the choice to either put the coffee cup aside with a little cool coffee left or get a "warm-up," I can keep running on empty, or get a spiritual "warm-up" — that is, a little spiritual fervor to get my juices flowing. Romans 12:11 says, "Never be lacking in zeal, but keep your spiritual fervor, serving the Lord" (NIV).

Merriam Webster defines fervor as "intense heat."[15] It also defines zeal as "eagerness and ardent interest in pursuit of something."[16] That almost gives a picture of Michelle going for that warm cup of coffee! How does a person keep her fervor? Different people have different ways. Some people read their Bibles and pray. I like to take a long drive and watch the blue sky. It's like the sky is a big canvas and God draws something new for me every day. How can seeing the beauty of His Almighty hand not make you want to do anything but worship him? If I listen to some good Christian music and drink some hot coffee along with that, look out world!

So, because you are lukewarm—neither hot nor cold—I am about to spit you out of my mouth.
Revelation 3:16 NIV

TAKE YOUR SHOES OFF!

Krista enjoys the activities that preschool offers, but her favorite activity is dressing up at playtime. Krista spends countless hours prancing around in her dress-up shoes at home, pretending that she is a princess. I allow her to wear the shoes for as long as she wants at home, but she has limited play time at preschool. After playing for a certain period of time, Krista's preschool teacher makes her put her shoes away so that the academic lessons can begin. Krista wasn't ready to take off her fancy dress-up shoes today, but the teacher insisted.

In Exodus 3:5, God commanded Moses to take off his shoes because he was standing on holy ground. In that day, removing shoes in worship was a common practice because the feet became dirty from walking in the dirt and sand. Deep down, Moses probably wanted to remain in these comfortable shoes, but Moses removed his shoes and followed the direction that God commanded.

God calls us to take off our shoes too. Like Moses, we must remove our shoes — the sin and things of our past that hold us back, and follow in the direction God leads.

"Do not come any closer," God said. "Take off your sandals, for the place where you are standing is holy ground."
Exodus 3:5, NIV

QUEEN OF THE HILL

What an encounter with the Creator this week! My family traveled to Stone Mountain, GA to encounter the majesty of Stone Mountain Park. At heights 1,686 feet above sea level, this huge granite mountain is a beauty to behold.[17] The carving on this mountain bears the images of Confederate leaders, Robert E. Lee, Jefferson Davis, and Stonewall Jackson.[18]

While visiting Stone Mountain, we took a train ride 3.5 miles around the mountain and hiked 1.3 miles to the top of the mountain. We huffed and puffed up the mountain, while Krista happily skipped along ahead of us. The last stretch was the most difficult, but there was a hand rail at the steepest point to keep our feet from slipping. We finally made it to the top! Although we were exhausted, the view was breathtaking, and the cool air was refreshing.

After taking a few pictures, I now faced a new dilemma — I had to descend from the mountain. I'm not fond of heights, so neither option appealed to me. Option one was to take the skyline, which was a cable car that scaled the mountain. Although I'm sure it was completely safe, I was afraid of the skyline. Option two was to hike back — 1.3 miles downhill. That didn't appeal to me because I could easily lose my step and slide downhill.

One thing was for sure — I could not stay on the mountain. Krista believed that "kabob cats" may live on that mountain at night, and I wasn't so sure that she was wrong! We were also low on water and getting a little hungry. We chose to descend the same way we ascended — by foot! I met another lady on the way down, who had not yet climbed the mountain and was asking questions about what to expect. We have mountain-top experiences in our Christian walk. Getting to the top of the mountain — the place where things are easy and refreshing, is hard. When we finally reach that place of contentment, we want to stay, but we can't stay there forever. Another valley will surely come along in a matter of time. It may be sickness, financial hardships, or conflict. We may have to descend from the mountain and deal with these troubles, but it is in the valley that God restores us and shapes us to be more like Him. He will be watching over you and will not let your foot slip. He may also use us to help others along the way.

I will lift up mine eyes unto the hills, from whence cometh my help. My help cometh from the LORD, which made heaven and earth. He will not suffer thy foot to be moved: he that keepeth thee will not slumber.
Psalm 121:1-3, KJV

SEVEN CENTS

A friend of mine has a 1½-year-old son who is going through a stage where he places everything in his mouth. His mother recently told me that she found seven cents in his mouth. I joked with her that this child has already learned to "put his money where his mouth is."

This story reminded me how our mouths can be valuable or invaluable, depending on the things we say and the way we say them. Proverbs 25:11 says, "A word fitly spoken is like apples of gold in pictures of silver" (KJV). Psalm 66:10 tells us that God refines us like silver. After God refines us, burning off all the impurities of the world, we become like fine silver that shows the reflection of our Maker. When we speak to people in an appropriate manner at the proper time, refraining from anger and harsh words, these words are like apples of gold in pictures of silver.

"A word fitly spoken is like apples of gold in pictures of silver."
Proverbs 25:11, KJV

CRAZY SUICIDAL SQUIRREL

I remember hearing my cousin yell, "You crazy suicidal squirrel!" as she swerved to miss the small furry creature that crossed the road in front of her car. To this day, I laugh every time a squirrel darts out in front of my car because I remember Betty's perfect description of the squirrel.

Squirrels will run out in the middle of the street and dart back and forth before finally crossing over. Squirrels have to be the most indecisive creatures that ever existed! I am pretty indecisive myself, which is a trait that my sister and I share. When we planned our parents' 50th wedding anniversary party and were discussing ideas, I would ask, "I don't know. What you think?" She would reply, "I don't know. It's up to you."

While driving this weekend, I saw a squirrel run out in front of my car. After thinking, "Crazy suicidal squirrel," I thought about how many Christians are like that squirrel. We are Christians, but don't know which way to go. We want to be followers of Christ, but still want to stand in the middle somewhere.

Like the squirrel, we go back and forth between what God wants and what the world wants. Christ calls us to stand up for Him in all we do. Revelation 3:15-16 says, "I know your deeds, that you are neither cold nor hot. I wish you were either one or the other! So, because you are lukewarm — neither hot nor cold — I am about to spit you out of my mouth" (NIV). God doesn't want us to sit in the middle. He wants us to have a holy passion for Him and to live the life that He wants us to live. It's hard to live that life at times — especially when you are faced with daily decisions to do the right thing. Whether at school or work, we are faced with the decision to take a stand as a

Christian, or to blend in with everyone else. Get out of the middle of the road, and don't be like that crazy suicidal squirrel.

I know your deeds, that you are neither cold nor hot. I wish you were either one or the other! So, because you are lukewarm—neither hot nor cold—I am about to spit you out of my mouth.
Revelation 3:15-16, NIV

THE PINK DRESS

For the past few months, Krista has admired a pretty, pink dress in the fabric department. Each time we passed the model dress, she would ask me to make her a dress just like it.

    I finally bought the fabric and began sewing the dress for her, but started sewing the dress late in the day. With each stitch, she grew more excited and asked how much longer it would be before she could wear the dress. I knew that she desperately hoped to wear her new dress to school the next day, so I stayed up past midnight sewing, ripping out stitches, and re-sewing until the dress was finished. As I wearily took care of the details, Krista slept peacefully, trusting that she would wake up to find a new dress that she could proudly show her friends.

As I sewed late into the night, God revealed to me His deep level of patience and His ability to take care of us. There was a time when I spent many sleepless nights worrying about the day or years to come. I finally realized that there is no need for sleepless nights caused by worry. Psalm 121:4 says, "Behold, he that keepeth Israel shall neither slumber nor sleep" (KJV).

While we sleep peacefully, God will be working out the details in our lives. While Krista slept peacefully, she had no guarantee that my project would be a success, but with God in charge, we know that it will turn out good.

And God saw every thing that he had made, and, behold, it was very good. And the evening and the morning were the sixth day.
Genesis 1:31, KJV

THE CREEPY HAND

I had a moment that I wish I had captured on video. I think it could have been a feature on one of the funniest pet videos. For some time, my home hasn't been cooling or heating well. Air conditioning specialists came to look at the problem, but they wanted to replace the ducts in our home, which came with a rather expensive price tag of around $2,000! Needless to say, we have put this off for quite some time. Mark finally decided to look underneath the house to determine the severity of the problem. When he climbed underneath the house, he found that two separate sections of the duct work had become completely detached from the air vents, so the air was just blowing into open space and not into our home.

The funniest part of this whole experience was watching as Mark worked to re-connect the air duct to the vent. My dog went berserk! She heard something beneath the house and couldn't figure out what kind of creature was down there making so much noise. All of a sudden, a hand reached up, popped the vent cover off, and waved around in our house. Daisy turned her head sideways and barked her head off. She was flipping out! We laughed and laughed.

This must have been how King Belshazzar felt when he saw the mysterious hand appear and write on the wall in Daniel 5. He was so terrified that his color changed and his knees started knocking — kind of like Daisy. Like our air duct connections, sometimes we can become disconnected from our power source and need a little repairing too. We try as we may, but just can't do anything on our own without the Lord. I feel this way quite often! That's when the Lord reaches out His hand and helps us back up. Sometimes, the repair isn't easy, but it's important nonetheless.

To this day, Daisy won't come too close to the vents in the house without thinking about the hand reaching up that day. I hope we will have Daisy's outlook and never forget the day that God reached down for us.

Fear thou not; for I am with thee: be not dismayed; for I am thy God: I will strengthen thee; yea, I will help thee; yea, I will uphold thee with the right hand of my righteousness.
Isaiah 41:10, KJV

THE BEARDED DRAGON

Earlier this week, I visited the pet store with Krista. We enjoyed looking at the bunnies, puppies, and hamsters, but what interested us most was the reptiles. The one that caught our attention was a creepy looking bearded dragon. While we watched him, he watched us like we were giant crickets. There he lay, without a care in the world, on top of a sticky cactus. I couldn't understand how he could lie on something so prickly and painful. A closer look revealed that the cactus was artificial. That creepy, little lizard didn't let the sticky cactus intimidate him. He crawled right on top of it and rested.

When times get stressful, take on the attitude of the bearded dragon — not intimidated by what seems to be a tough situation. Ask God for wisdom and for strength to persevere. There's rest at the top of the mountain.

Consider it pure joy, my brothers and sisters, whenever you face trials of many kinds, because you know that the testing of your faith produces perseverance. Let perseverance finish its work so that you may be mature and complete, not lacking anything. If any of you lacks wisdom, you should ask God, who gives generously to all without finding fault, and it will be given to you.
James 1:2-5, NIV

PANELED HOUSES

My family was excited to relocate to the place we now call home. We have been living with my parents while we search for our own home. Choosing the perfect home is no easy task. We don't know much about home repairs, so we are seeking a newer home that will require fewer repairs and updates. One of the older homes we viewed was built in 1961. Although this house had great potential, it would require a lot of hard work. The entire living room, including the fireplace, was made of pine-paneled walls. My brother-in-law told us that pine-paneled walls are a very nice feature and were highly treasured in earlier days, but the color of the wood made the house seem dark and lonely.

Picking up my Bible tonight, I read Haggai 1:4, "Is it a time for you yourselves to be living in your paneled houses, while this house remains a ruin?" (NIV) For the past few weeks, I've become so consumed with our move and finding a new home that my spiritual house has become a ruin. Whatever home I buy will probably be unsightly to someone 50 years from now, but my spiritual house will live forever in the presence of the Almighty God. I hope to leave a legacy for generations to come.

"Is it a time for you yourselves to be living in your paneled houses, while this house remains a ruin?"
Haggai 1:4, NIV

THE BUTTERFLY

The Viceroy butterfly is a very clever insect. It so closely resembles the Monarch butterfly that it is often mistaken for one. Birds are a threat to butterflies, but God gave the Viceroy butterfly the ability to outwit its predators. *Henderson State University* explains that the Viceroy is a "mimic." "If a bird eats a Monarch butterfly, the toxic plant glycosides stored in the butterfly make the bird sick. The bird may vomit but does not die. Remembering the color pattern of the butterfly, the bird learns from the experience and no longer is interested in eating Monarchs."[19]

    I recently had a medical procedure that I dreaded. Fearful thoughts passed through my mind the day before the procedure. With much prayer, dependence on God for courage, and quoting memorized scripture, I had perfect peace the day of the procedure. When we feel that we aren't strong enough or brave enough, we should follow the example of the Viceroy butterfly — not relying on how strong we are, or what we can do, but relying on what we can do through Christ.

I know what it is to be in need, and I know what it is to have plenty. I have learned the secret of being content in any and every situation, whether well fed or hungry, whether living in plenty or in want. I can do all this through him who gives me strength.
Philippians 4:12-13, NIV

NO PASTURE

I can always tell when I am not having enough quality time with God. I become very grouchy, unhappy, and dissatisfied. After I finally recognize the problem and spend some much needed time with God, I am happy and pleasant again.

The book of Joel describes how the beasts groan and the herds of cattle are perplexed because they have no pasture. God also wants us to make time with Him every day to find the rest and spiritual nourishment that He offers.

How do the beasts groan! the herds of cattle are perplexed, because they have no pasture; yea, the flocks of sheep are made desolate.
Joel 1:18, KJV

THE 71-NIGHT REVIVAL

Many years ago, my grandpa was preaching a revival at a church where my parents first met. This was no ordinary revival, but a 71-night revival! My dad said that when he saw my mom on the first night, he climbed in the window to sit beside her. He thought she was the prettiest girl there, and he just had to meet her. He did not miss a single night of the 71-night revival — not because he enjoyed the preaching, but because he longed to be with the woman of his dreams. That is true devotion!

Are we so committed to God that we would show our desire for Him? Would we do whatever it takes to spend 71 uninterrupted evenings with Him?

Be kindly affectioned one to another with brotherly love; in honour preferring one another; Not slothful in business; fervent in spirit; serving the Lord...
Romans 12:10-11, KJV

COME AND DINE

Krista loves to play restaurant. After having lunch with my family at a restaurant, she brought home a few paper place mats to play with. She asked me to come and play restaurant with her, but since it had been a busy day and I was tired, I told her that I would play with her the next day instead. After she went to bed, I came in the room to discover a small table covered with a purple zebra-print cloth, two paper place mats, two plates, and two cups with two straws. There were also two plastic forks wrapped with napkins that were beautifully garnished with a white piece of yarn tied in a bow. It broke my heart that I had been too tired and busy to dine with my favorite little girl and share a special moment with her.

God reminded me that although He desires my company, I'm often too tired or busy to spend time with Him too. Like the table that Krista had spread, God also has a table spread, as the old gospel hymn goes, "Jesus has a table spread, where the saints of God are fed, he invites his chosen people, 'come and dine.' With His manna, He doth feed, and supplies our every need: Oh, 'tis sweet to sup with Jesus all the time!'"[20]

Jesus saith unto them, Come and Dine. And none of the disciples durst ask him, Who art thou? knowing that it was the Lord.
John 21:12, KJV

THE FALLEN TREE

A 60-foot-tall Ficus tree fell in our backyard during a strong hurricane. It could have seriously damaged our home, but we were blessed that it fell in the opposite direction. The root system of this tree was amazing. The main root extended approximately 25-feet-long and was four inches thick. Tree roots tend to grow toward sources of water. We too, should be rooted deeply in Christ for our source of refreshment and strength in strong storms.

That he would grant you, according to the riches of his glory, to be strengthened with might by his Spirit in the inner man; That Christ may dwell in your hearts by faith; that ye, being rooted and grounded in love, May be able to comprehend with all saints what is the breadth, and length, and depth, and height; And to know the love of Christ, which passeth knowledge, that ye might be filled with all the fulness of God.
Ephesians 3:16-19, KJV

WALKING PARTNERS

My friend Suzanne and I walked daily at a large park that encircled the building where we worked. After work, we would put on our walking shoes and share many laughs and stories with each other as we walked around the park. It was a great way to relieve the stress that we endured at work and a fun way to exercise. We shared times of happiness and times of heartache.

We had planned to walk one day, but I forgot my walking shoes. I didn't want to miss walking with my friend, so I hiked the trail in boots. By the end of our walk, my feet were killing me, and there was an obstacle which caused a long detour. It was dark when we finally returned to our cars. Suzanne and I walked daily until the week that I went on maternity leave. Medical reports show that walking helps with child birth and I believe that's true.

As Christians, we should also stay fit — spiritually fit. We have a partner to help us on our journey too. As the old hymn goes, *"And he walks with me, and he talks with me, and he tells me I am his own, and the joy we share as we tarry there, none other has ever known."*[21] Like my walking partner, the Lord will never leave us. When we are too tired to make it, He even carries us.

The New International Version so beautifully says in Isaiah 46:4, "Even to your old age and gray hairs I am he, I am he who will sustain you. I have made you and I will carry you; I will sustain you and I will rescue you" (NIV). He is our friend, comforter, confidant, joy, and salvation. He is our light in the darkness. If we spend time daily with Him, we are sure to be ready when we need Him the most.

He gives strength to the weary and increases the power of the weak. Even youths grow tired and weary, and young men stumble and fall; but those who hope in the LORD will renew their strength. They will soar on wings like eagles; they will run and not grow weary, they will walk and not be faint.
Isaiah 40:29-31, NIV

THE CICADA

Krista and I were exploring one day when we discovered an empty Cicada (locust) shell on a tree. Thinking that this would be a great way to teach Krista about death, I explained that the human body is like a Cicada shell. When a Christian dies, the body remains, but the spirit goes to be with Jesus in Heaven. As an example, I explained how my Uncle Leo left his earthly body behind like the Cicada shell, while his spirit went away to be with Jesus. I burst into laughter as she pointed to the bug and questioned, "Is that Uncle Leo?"

The Australian Museum reports that nymphs, which are wingless Cicadas, "fall to the ground and burrow below the surface. Here they live on sap from plant roots for a period which may last several years. They shed their skin at intervals as they grow. When the nymph reaches full size it digs its way to the surface with its front legs...The nymph then climbs on a tree trunk or other object and sheds its skin for the last time. The fully-winged adult cicada which emerges leaves its old empty nymphal skin behind."[22]

I've had quite a few disappointments lately where people I've trusted and admired have disappointed me. With each disappointment, God has taught me that I put too much faith in man and not enough faith in God. People will sin and, as a Christian, I must forgive their actions as God forgives mine. Christians are like the growing nymph, which slowly sheds its skin a little at a time and leaves its old self behind. Feeding on the power of the Holy Spirit, the Christian's purpose is to grow and mature, and reach the level where he leaves his old ways behind and becomes a new person.

Who his own self bare our sins in his own body on the tree, that we, being dead to sins, should live unto righteousness: by whose stripes ye were healed.
1 Peter 2:24, KJV

MOON STRUCK

We were driving home from a fall festival about an hour away from home. While driving home, Krista took the opportunity to seek out "Dannaw's star." Her grandma, whom she calls "Dannaw," told Krista that she would know her star because it's the brightest star in the sky. Tonight, she didn't see Dannaw's star, but she was amazed by the big, bright moon. She said "Mama, do you ever notice how the moon looks like it moves when we turn left or right?" "Yes," I told her. "As a matter of fact, I remember asking my mom the same thing when I was a child." I explained to Krista that although the moon appears to move when the car changes directions, it actually remains in the same exact spot.

God reminded me of my own life and how He remained constant when I wondered where He was. In times when I didn't feel His presence or hear His voice, He had not changed or moved away, but I had. He had remained with me all along, just as the moon remains in the same location. He still shows me His love every day, but I am often too busy to see Him.

And ye shall seek me, and find me, when ye shall search for me with all your heart.
Jeremiah 29:13, KJV

THE DOVES

As I watch the doves on the bird feeder in my backyard, I am encouraged by their determination. There are so many spilled seed on the ground below that it would be much easier to feed from the ground. Instead, the doves struggle to fit their huge bodies on the tiny feeder and spin repeatedly — flapping their wings to stay seated.

When Jesus and His disciples went to the home of Martha, she was so busy making preparations for her guests that she became stressed and struggled to get things done. Mary just sat at Jesus' feet, listening to His every word. Jesus told Martha that she was worried and upset about many things, but Mary had chosen the better thing to do. Sometimes we struggle to do too much when Jesus only wants us to sit and meditate on Him.

And Jesus answered and said unto her, Martha, Martha, thou art careful and troubled about many things: But one thing is needful: and Mary hath chosen that good part, which shall not be taken away from her.
Luke 10:41-42, KJV

STUCK IN THE MUD

My family attended a little church in the woods for a homecoming service. It had been raining hard, and we knew that the dirt roads were bad on the way to church, but they had deteriorated even more by the time we left to drive home. During the homecoming lunch, someone told us of an "easier" route to take — off the beaten path. When we left the church, we took the gentleman's advice and turned left. Everything seemed to be going well – for a short time! We got about 300 feet from the main road when we started up a hill and got stuck in the mud. Instead of stopping at that point and looking for help, we decided to put the truck in reverse. That made it even worse, and we ended up on the very edge of a ditch filled with flowing mud. Mark couldn't get out of the truck on his side because of the ditch, so he crawled out my door and walked through the mud and rain to find help. Our mobile phones couldn't hold a signal in the woods, and we knew we were in big trouble. If we had taken the other route perhaps someone could find us, but who would come by this way?

As Mark looked for help, he worried that the muddy waters might wash the truck away while he was gone. A few minutes later, I saw Mark walking toward us, followed by a man driving a big tractor. I felt like a lost kid at an amusement park, who had been discovered by her family. The kind gentleman hooked our truck up to his tractor and dragged us out of the mud and onto the paved road a few hundred feet ahead. He asked which direction we were going and set our truck in that direction.

This is a perfect picture of Psalm 40:1-2. "I waited patiently for the LORD; and he inclined unto me, and heard my cry. He brought me up also out of an horrible pit, out of the miry clay, and set my feet upon a rock, and established my goings" (KJV).

Like the man on the tractor, God hears our cries and is able to bring us up out of the pit — out of the miry clay. The pit and miry clay can be anything you are struggling with — sin, depression, health problems, financial difficulties, or relationships. When we try to do things ourselves, we only make things worse. That is usually the point when we cry out to God for help. Like the tractor that pulled us up out of the mud and onto the paved road, God sets our feet upon a rock and establishes the way we should go.

I waited patiently for the LORD; and he inclined unto me, and heard my cry. He brought me up also out of an horrible pit, out of the miry clay, and set my feet upon a rock, and established my goings.
Psalm 40:1-2, KJV

SCARLETT, THE OTHER WOMAN!

Scarlett is the other woman in my husband's life. She's "red" and has a great body. She's 35, but looks great for her age, although she has definitely had some work done. Before I get you too concerned about my husband's faithfulness, let me just say that Scarlett is a smoking hot, red 1976 BMW 2002.

I call her Scarlett because of her color, but I refer to her as "the other woman" because of how much time he spends working on her. She didn't always look this good. Last spring, Mark spent several weeks restoring her body. She had rust in some places and some serious peeling issues.

Mark spent several weeks just scraping and grinding to remove the rust spots. Then he began patching and sanding before he finally started with the painting process. I just knew that he was going to ruin the car. Though the prep work was a long and grueling process, it was necessary. Without removing the rust, the car's body would have only deteriorated further. Without sanding, the paint wouldn't adhere to the car.

There are times in life when I feel like I'm in God's body shop. I don't have much patience with waiting for the work in progress. He uses trials in my life to dig out the imperfections, lack of faith, or sinful ways, and smooth them to perfection. The sanding and digging can, at times, be extremely painful, but almost always results in a new and improved me! My new appearance will better reflect the image of my Detailer.

Beloved, think it not strange concerning the fiery trial which is to try you, as though some strange thing happened unto you: But rejoice, inasmuch as ye are partakers of Christ's sufferings; that, when his glory shall be revealed, ye may be glad also with exceeding joy.
1 Peter 4:12-13, KJV

THE FLYING ANTS

I love to see all of God's creation, but I want to see it through a window where all the creepy crawlers can't get to me. I am terrified of snakes, lizards, frogs, spiders, and other lurking bugs that are just waiting for a chance to pounce on me. It's like they have their own sense of humor and when they see me, they signal to their friends, "ATTACK!"

Just yesterday, my family visited our health club's pool and, for some reason, the pool and air was full of flying ants. As if regular ants aren't bad enough, these ants had wings and could not only crawl, but also swim and fly. Just as soon as I got in the pool water, "ATTACK!" Krista and I immediately jumped out of the water and darted through all the flying bombers — into the spraying fountains. Surprisingly, the ants were fairly limited in that area. They were thriving in the still waters, but they didn't want to be near the rushing waters.

In John 4:14, Jesus was telling the lady at the well about living water. When she asked where she could get the living water, He answered, "But whosoever drinketh of the water that I shall give him shall never thirst; but the water that I shall give him shall be in him a well of water springing up into everlasting life" (KJV). Living water springing up must have sounded wonderful to this lady. No more drawing water out of a deep hole, but instead a spring, bubbling up with fresh water!

The lesson in both my story of the ants and the story of the lady at the well is to not remain in still waters. We want to be in flowing springs of living water. We need to progress in Christian growth. 1 Peter 5:8 says, "Be sober, be vigilant; because your adversary the devil, as a roaring lion, walketh about, seeking whom he may devour" (KJV).

Ephesians 6:16 tells us how to be prepared. "Above all, taking the shield of faith, wherewith ye shall be able to quench all the fiery darts of the wicked" (KJV).

But whosoever drinketh of the water that I shall give him shall never thirst; but the water that I shall give him shall be in him a well of water springing up into everlasting life.
John 4:14, KJV

PATTERN

When Krista was younger, I enjoyed making pretty dresses for her. Sewing can be frustrating, yet very rewarding when your design is finished. Some patterns are more complex than others, depending on your level of experience. If you don't follow the pattern exactly, you can easily end up with a mess. I've threatened many times to throw my sewing machine into the canal behind my house — not because the machine doesn't work, but because the operator doesn't know how to use it.

Jesus came to Earth to teach us and set an example to live by. He is the perfect pattern, and we should strive to live our lives as He would. One way to do this is to constantly ask ourselves what He would do in every situation. As Christians, we want to try to be a replica of Christ, so that others will see Him living in us. Now I must go rip out these stitches and start sewing again!

Looking unto Jesus the author and finisher of our faith; who for the joy that was set before him endured the cross, despising the shame, and is set down at the right hand of the throne of God.
Hebrews 12:2, KJV

THE GARAGE SALE

I love garage sale shopping, but I can only occasionally drag myself out of bed early enough to go. I remember shopping at a garage sale a few years ago when a lady was extremely competitive with me over a shop vacuum that we both saw for $10. Mark had wanted one for a long time, but we didn't want to pay a lot of money for one. The lady started arguing with me that she had seen the vacuum first. My mom thought she was going to have to break up a fight between the lady and me. I'm happy to say that I brought the vacuum home. What the lady didn't realize is that I had already purchased the vacuum from the seller.

Satan tries to quarrel with us in the same way. He tries to make us feel like we have lost the battle. When he tells us these lies, we can boldly tell him to flee because Jesus paid the price a long time ago, and the victory belongs to us. That shop vacuum has cleaned up many messes throughout the years, and I feel that God has cleaned up many messes in my life too!

But thanks be to God, which giveth us the victory through our Lord Jesus Christ.
1 Corinthians 15:57, KJV

THE OYSTER

When Krista was younger, I bought her a jewelry kit containing a shell with a pearl inside. She opened the can and picked out the pearl, which she placed inside a silver-colored necklace.

Pearls are formed inside oysters, but the process is very uncomfortable for the oyster. Most pearls are made from a parasite that embeds in the oyster's soft tissue. *HowStuffWorks* explains, "The formation of a natural pearl begins when a foreign substance slips into the oyster between the mantle and the shell, which irritates the mantle. It's kind of like the oyster getting a splinter. The oyster's natural reaction is to cover up that irritant to protect itself. The mantle covers the irritant with layers of the same nacre substance that is used to create the shell. This eventually forms a pearl."[23]

We also must face trials and discomforts that sometimes seem to last forever. In these difficult times, we must continue to wrap ourselves with the promises of God. Eventually, despite the hardships, we become stronger through Christ, and the hardship is replaced with a blessing. Like the oyster, we can take an uncomfortable situation and replace it with something beautiful.

Consider it pure joy, my brothers and sisters, whenever you face trials of many kinds, because you know that the testing of your faith produces perseverance. Let perseverance finish its work so that you may be mature and complete, not lacking anything.
James 1:2-4, NIV

TRUE LOVE

I recently read a story of a young couple preparing for their wedding. On the day of their wedding, a terrible tsunami hit, and they were separated for days. The wedding was slightly delayed, but their love carried them through, and they were married a few weeks later.

True love cannot be drowned, even by the ocean's strongest waves. This true love is found in Jesus Christ. Romans 8:38-39 tells us, "For I am persuaded, that neither death, nor life, nor angels, nor principalities, nor powers, nor things present, nor things to come, Nor height, nor depth, nor any other creature, shall be able to separate us from the love of God, which is in Christ Jesus our Lord" (KJV). Right now we are in the same period of transition as the young couple — waiting for a short period of time until our bridegroom returns for us.

Many waters cannot quench love, neither can the floods drown it: if a man would give all the substance of his house for love, it would utterly be contemned.
Song of Solomon 8:7, KJV

SWEET NECTAR

My mom and aunt are both hummingbird lovers. They faithfully fill their feeders with red sugar water known as nectar and watch the hummingbirds feed all day. The hummingbirds are attracted to the feeder by the color of the nectar. Once they taste the nectar, they see that it is good and feed on it all day.

Like the attractive color of the nectar, how we live as Christians may attract or repel others. If they see good fruit, they will want to sup too, but if they see no fruit or bad fruit, they may not want to taste and see that the Lord is good.

O taste and see that the LORD is good: blessed is the man that trusteth in him.
Psalm 34:8, KJV

TELLING SENTENCES

I enjoy volunteering in Krista's reading group and watching the children as they learn to read and write. The teacher has been explaining to the class the difference between "question sentences" and "telling sentences." The teacher gave the children an assignment and told them to circle the "telling sentence." The kids had a difficult time understanding which sentence told a story and which sentence asked a question. Finally, I asked one of the students, "If I were to say to you, 'Sam, does your dog dig?' would that be an asking sentence or a telling sentence?" When I addressed Sam by his name and made it personal, he suddenly understood and was able to answer the questions.

This is how it is with studying the Word of God. The pages of the Bible may not have much meaning alone, but the Holy Spirit is there to make it personal — whispering words of wisdom to help us comprehend what we are reading, and guiding us in what is right.

Sam now understands the difference between question sentences and telling sentences because of the personal application involved. We can understand what God is teaching us because He teaches us new things every day. We only have to listen for that still, small voice.

These things have I spoken unto you, being yet present with you. But the Comforter, which is the Holy Ghost, whom the Father will send in my name, he shall teach you all things, and bring all things to your remembrance, whatsoever I have said unto you.
John 14:25-26, KJV

THE SPRAYED CAT

I spend a lot of time watching the birds and squirrels feed from my bird feeders throughout the day. What I do not like is the cat that uses my feeders as a trap to catch birds. Krista doesn't like the cat either and told me that she wishes Jesus would just take the cat to Heaven. "Why?" I asked. She said, "Because I don't like him trying to catch the birds and squirrels." Krista's attitude was much more loving than mine. I sought revenge and sprayed the cat out of the yard with a water hose that was turned on full-blast. My victory was only brief because as soon as I turned off the water and dropped the hose, the hose sprayed me!

Too often, we are more interested in seeking revenge than we are in helping others. In the Bible, Jacob loved his son Joseph more than his other sons and even made him a beautiful robe to show his love. Joseph shared a dream with his brothers in which his brothers' sheaves of grain were bowing down to his. Joseph's brothers burned with anger and hatred toward Joseph and sought revenge by selling Joseph to the Ishmaelites and deceiving their father into thinking that Joseph had been killed by a ferocious animal.

The brothers' actions seemed victorious at first. Although Joseph was out of the picture and sold as a slave to serve others, God used the deceitfulness of the brothers to put Joseph in a position of leadership. In the middle of a great famine, Joseph's brothers went down to Egypt to buy food and found that the one they tried to get rid of was now in a position of great importance. Joseph had become the governor of Egypt! The brothers would have to bow down to Joseph as predicted in the dream. Instead of seeking revenge, we should show love and allow God to judge the actions of others.

Do not be overcome by evil, but overcome evil with good.
Romans 12:21, NIV

SWEET TOOTH

Christmas is over and the new year has begun. If you're like me, you have made the declaration that all the overeating is over! That is — until after lunch or dinner when that sweet tooth starts screaming for some pumpkin pie or red velvet cake. Today I tried to calm my sweet craving with soft peppermint candy, thinking that it would be less fattening and still satisfy my sweet craving. My taste buds didn't agree. Instead, I broke down and bought a donut at the supermarket.

People were made with a physical hunger, but we were also made with a spiritual hunger. Our heart longs for constant fellowship with God. Instead, we seek to fill ourselves with the physical by cramming every activity and source of enjoyment that we possibly can into our busy schedules. At the end of the day, we may devote five minutes in prayer or study. No wonder we are so tired and frustrated! Keep on track with your physical diet, but over-indulge on your spiritual diet.

Oh that men would praise the LORD for his goodness, and for his wonderful works to the children of men! For he satisfieth the longing soul, and filleth the hungry soul with goodness.
Psalm 107:8-9, KJV

THE BLANKET

> ...THE LORD KNOWETH THEM THAT ARE HIS...
> II TIMOTHY 2:19

For the past few days, my mother has been working on a project that God put on her heart. She felt that God wanted her to prepare a small, lightweight blanket to give to a friend in the nursing home. She purchased a piece of lightweight fabric and gently stitched around the edges. My mom wanted her friend to have this blanket to cover up with, but also to remind her that God would always remember her — no matter what!

I helped my mom with the final touches of the blanket, which was an iron-on transfer of part of a verse, "The Lord knoweth them that are his...." It has been on my mom's heart in the past few months that when people are older or in nursing homes, their memories often fail. They may not remember their loved ones, and sometimes it may seem that people they used to see all the time have forgotten them. Even in these times, God will never forget our names, or anything about us. We are his beloved children, and he spoke us into existence — planning out every single detail of our lives. Psalm 139:13 says, "thou has covered me in my mother's womb" (KJV).

While ironing on this transfer, we had to keep pressing the hot iron over the same word that wouldn't stick to the fabric. Ironically, the part of the word that wouldn't stick was "K-N-O-W." We wondered why only those four letters wouldn't stick. I personally think that God was trying to teach us that "knowing" something in life doesn't always stick with us, and we may still doubt what we "know" is true.

The Israelites knew full well the things that God had brought them through in the wilderness. God even parted the Red Sea for them, yet they constantly doubted! We know that God promises us in Hebrews 13:5, "Never will I leave you; never will I forsake you" (NIV), but we still doubt. My mom and I had to constantly press the word "KNOW" over and over again, just as we have to constantly press these precious promises of God on our hearts. Keep the precious words of God close to your heart and *know* that He meant every word that was written!

Nevertheless the foundation of God standeth sure, having this seal, The Lord knoweth them that are his. And, let every one that nameth the name of Christ depart from iniquity.
2 Timothy 2:19, KJV

THE BIG OAK

Thomasville, Georgia is home to one of the largest oak trees in the United States. The *Thomasville Visitor's Center* reports, "Now over 325 years old, the Big Oak has a limb span of over 165 feet and a trunk circumference of over 26 feet."[24]

When I first saw the tree, I was amazed by its enormous size. The tree is so large that the leaves of its branches brush the ground. These branches rely upon cables for support. The fern greenery that grows on the tree is called a "resurrection fern." *Thomasville Visitor's Center* explains that the fern "is called the 'resurrection fern' because it appears dead until a rain causes it to turn immediately to a lush green."[25] No doubt this tree has weathered many storms! As old as the tree is, it is a beautiful and amazing sight.

Isaiah 61:3 references the mourners in Zion as "oaks of righteousness, a planting of the LORD for the display of his splendor" (NIV). When the Israelites were in battle against Amelek in Exodus 17:8-16, the Israelites prevailed as long as Moses held up his hand. When his hand was too heavy to remain outstretched, Aaron & Hur held Moses' hand up, and he was steady until the sun went down.

Just as the Big Oak's outstretched branches are strengthened by the cables, the Israelite army was only strong because of God's power working through them. Like the branches of the Big Oak, we must depend on God — even when our faith is stretched to its limits.

...and provide for those who grieve in Zion — to bestow on them a crown of beauty instead of ashes, the oil of gladness instead of mourning, and a garment of praise instead of a spirit of despair. They will be called oaks of righteousness, a planting of the LORD for the display of his splendor.
Isaiah 61:3, NIV

ONE WAY STREET

After work, I drove my car out of the parking garage and began the long drive home. I had a good day at work, but it's always a good feeling to get in the car and go home.

I'd driven these roads for years, but for some reason, I turned too soon and ended up on a one-way street — going the wrong way! By that time, it was too late to turn around because there was an on-coming car approaching. I wouldn't have time to throw the gear in reverse and turn around. I had no choice but to zoom forward and pray that I would be safe. Cars in both lanes were approaching, but I quickly took a right-hand turn and got on a safe road. Whew!

This little incident reminded me of how many people are on the wrong road in life. In the Sermon on the Mount, Jesus taught this when He said, "Enter through the narrow gate. For wide is the gate and broad is the road that leads to destruction, and many enter through it. But small is the gate and narrow the road that leads to life, and only a few find it" (Matthew 7:13-14, NIV).

No matter what people may tell you, the Bible says there is only one way to the Father and that is through Jesus Christ.

For there is one God, and one mediator between God and men, the man Christ Jesus; Who gave himself a ransom for all, to be testified in due time.
1 Timothy 2:5-6, KJV

THE BALL THIEF

Krista learned a scripture memory game at church that we enjoy playing at home. We sit across from each other on the floor and throw a tennis ball to each other. With each throw we say a Bible verse — one word at a time. This helps us remember the verse and provides entertainment for our feisty dachshund.

Daisy could spend hours playing ball, so this is her favorite time of the day. As we throw the ball to each other and say the verse one word at a time, Daisy jumps between us and tries to catch the ball while it's up in the air. If she catches the ball, we have to start the verse all over again. Daisy can steal the ball and ruin a good game, but we just start over again and repeat the verse, word-by-word.

God's word is a powerful weapon, sharper than any double-edged sword. Isaiah 55:11-12 says, "So shall my word be that goeth forth out of my mouth: it shall not return unto me void, but it shall accomplish that which I please, and it shall prosper in the thing whereto I sent it. For ye shall go out with joy, and be led forth with peace: the mountains and the hills shall break forth before you into singing, and all the trees of the field shall clap their hands" (KJV).

Satan may steal our momentary happiness with the things that he throws our way, but with God's Word engraved on our heart and on our tongues, we have hope and joy beyond all understanding. We can pick up and start all over again.

For the word of God is quick, and powerful, and sharper than any twoedged sword, piercing even to the dividing asunder of soul and spirit, and of the joints and marrow, and is a discerner of the thoughts and intents of the heart.
Hebrews 4:12, KJV

THE GARDEN SNAKE

I attended a birthday party for a boy turning seven-years-old. It was a great party with all kinds of exciting activities for the kids, but the main attraction was peeking out of the pine straw surrounding a tall tree. We watched a small garden snake peek out with curiosity and caution. The snake was not dangerous, but I'll stand by my mother's philosophy that, "The only good snake is a dead snake." Nevertheless, we watched as the snake circled the tree and went back into its hole. It wasn't long before the children became aware of the snake and drew closer to catch a glimpse. As one boy got closer, the snake charged out to threaten him and then returned to its hole.

This event reminded me of the story of Moses. In his own strength, Moses was no more threatening than this garden snake. When God appeared to Moses in the burning bush, Moses gave several reasons why he should not be the one to deliver the Israelites out of Egypt. He lived a simple life as a shepherd. Have you ever noticed how God used shepherds for very important missions? Moses used every excuse not to go, but with every reluctant question, God gave a definite answer.

In Exodus 4, God told Moses to throw his staff on the ground. When he did, the staff became a snake. It doesn't say what kind of snake, but unless Moses shared my mother's philosophy, it must have been a dangerous snake. Moses then used his first act of faith in God by reaching down his hand and taking the snake by its tail. This would have been the most dangerous way to pick up a snake because the snake could have curled around to bite Moses. Upon picking up the snake, it became a staff again.

We can learn much from the garden snake and Moses. Although we know that we have no great power and are very little on our own, we must sometimes step into that area of uncertainty, depending on God to be our strength. The snake knew it was no match for this boy — especially surrounded by a large crowd of people. Moses needed strength too. It was only by faith in God that Moses not only had the courage to pick up the snake, but more importantly, the faith to take on Pharaoh and lead the Israelites out of bondage.

And God said unto Moses, I AM THAT I AM: and he said, Thus shalt thou say unto the children of Israel, I AM hath sent me unto you.
Exodus 3:14, KJV

THE LIBERTY BELL

The Liberty Bell is one of the most famous pieces of US history. Introduced in 1752, this nearly 2,000-pound bell has encouraged many people throughout the world. The Liberty Bell contains the Biblical message, "Proclaim LIBERTY throughout all the Land unto all the inhabitants thereof," taken from Leviticus 25:10. According to the *National Park Service*, "By 1846 a thin crack began to affect the sound of the bell. The bell was repaired in 1846 and rang for a George Washington birthday celebration, but the bell cracked again and has not been rung since. No one knows why the bell cracked either time."[26]

Although some would consider the Liberty Bell useless because of the crack, this imperfection did not decrease the value of the bell. Having paid equivalent to $225 US dollars for the bell, this piece of US history is now priceless. It is through brokenness that we also become priceless. It was through Jesus' broken body that our salvation became priceless. When the curtain of the temple was torn in two, our worship with God became priceless. God can use whatever brokenness you have suffered in life to make you priceless too. It is through brokenness that we are made whole. We are free in Christ.

At that moment the curtain of the temple was torn in two from top to bottom. The earth shook, the rocks split and the tombs broke open. The bodies of many holy people who had died were raised to life.
Matthew 27:51-52, NIV

THE GREAT FIND

My cousin Betty is one of the wisest shoppers I know. She shops at all the sales, searching long and hard for the perfect buy. She can detect a bargain and see its potential, despite its defects. Her most recent purchase was a pair of sterling silver cross earrings that she gave to me as a gift. The earrings were exactly my style, and I was anxious to wear them, but they were covered in tarnish. I'm sure many shoppers passed by these earrings, believing that they were beyond repair. Instead, they would likely choose a shiny pair without tarnish. Seeing potential, Betty purchased the earrings. After removing the tarnish, the earrings were spotless and shined like perfect silver.

This is how God sees us. Although our lives are tarnished with sin, he saw the potential for us. Through Jesus' death on the cross, He purchased us, regardless of our condition. Jesus' shed blood purified us and we have been washed clean. I now proudly wear my silver cross earrings. They are a constant reminder of my redemption by my Savior despite my flaws, my cleansed life through the cross, and how I am made to reflect the image of Him. Like the silver earrings, my life can appear tarnished with sin, but through Christ, I am never beyond repair.

And they sung a new song, saying, Thou art worthy to take the book, and to open the seals thereof: for thou wast slain, and hast redeemed us to God by thy blood out of every kindred, and tongue, and people, and nation...
Revelation 5:9, KJV

WHISPERING WITH GOD

Years ago, I wrote a song about my grandpa, who is now in Heaven. In this song, I referred to him as one of God's disciples. When I was young, I always believed that Grandpa was a disciple because I always saw him reading his Bible and thought that he was whispering to his Bible as he read the words in a soft whisper. As an adult, I now realize that Grandpa was in deep communion with God.

Just as Grandpa whispered the words, Jesus communicates with us by whispering to our hearts — often while we are studying our Bibles, praying, listening to Christian music, enjoying nature, and many other ways. God was whispering to Grandpa, while Grandpa was whispering to Him.

What I tell you in the dark, speak in the daylight; what is whispered in your ear, proclaim from the roofs.
Matthew 10:27, NIV

THE MUSIC ASSIGNMENT

Krista's violin teacher asked her students to compose a piece of music. I watched as Krista filled in the lines of the music staff with a treble clef, two sharp symbols, and some dangling notes. Confused, I asked why she would compose the music without first knowing what the song would sound like on the violin. I didn't realize that some of the greatest musical composers wrote the songs before they were ever played on an instrument. These classical composers already knew what the song would sound like before it was ever played.

By the age of 26, Ludwig van Beethoven began losing his hearing. According to *Wikipedia*, "Beethoven was almost completely deaf when he composed his ninth symphony."[27] It also reports that according to violinist, Joseph Böhm, "Beethoven directed the piece himself; that is, he stood before the lectern and gesticulated furiously. At times he rose, at other times he shrank to the ground, he moved as if he wanted to play all the instruments himself and sing for the whole chorus...."[28] It's as though he could feel the emotion of the music, even though he couldn't hear what was being played.

The audience just loved Beethoven. *Wikipedia* continues, "The whole audience acclaimed him through standing ovations five times; there were handkerchiefs in the air, hats, raised hands, so that Beethoven, who could not hear the applause, could at least see the ovation gestures."[29] The audience wanted Beethoven to see its gestures because he couldn't hear the applause.

When I first started playing music on the church praise team, I was learning to play a new instrument. After each mistake, I would feel defeated and say, "I can't do this!" Our worship leader called me to the side and told me, "Amy, you can play this instrument, but first you must have some confidence!" I have carried this piece of advice with me for years now. Whether playing music, going on an interview, or taking on a large assignment, I find that I can accomplish more when I start with a little faith.

Some of the greatest composers of all time wrote the music before an instrument was ever used. Sometimes we have to *know* before we can *see*. "Now faith is the substance of things hoped for, the evidence of things not seen" (Hebrews 11:1, KJV).

Some of the greatest Bible stories involved God using some very unqualified people to accomplish great things. When we feel that we can't do something because we can't see the end result, we need to step out on faith and believe that we can do these things with God's help!

I can do all things through Christ which strengtheneth me.
Philippians 4:13, KJV

WORTHLESS TREASURES

We took Krista to an amusement park with different animals and rides. She was so excited about going that she ran to her bedroom and brought back several small toys to take with her. I explained to her that once she saw all the exciting things at the park, she wouldn't care about the toys that she wanted to bring from home. Because she has never been to an amusement park, she didn't understand all the activities that the park would offer.

Just as Krista didn't understand the insignificance of her small toys in relation to the amusement park, sometimes we put too much value on the things we own or want to own. We go through life trying to acquire all that we can — the career of our dreams, a nice home, and money in the bank. The things we have here are like the little toys that Krista wanted to take to the amusement park. We don't seek God as our source of joy and fulfillment, or know how rich we are just to know Him. Instead, we treasure the physical things that we have on Earth and accumulate all that we can.

It makes little sense to worry about the little things that we have here on Earth because even if we could take them with us to Heaven, they would be as insignificant to us as Krista's small toys.

Lay not up for yourselves treasures upon earth, where moth and rust doth corrupt, and where thieves break through and steal: But lay up for yourselves treasures in heaven, where neither moth nor rust doth corrupt, and where thieves do not break through nor steal: For where your treasure is, there will your heart be also.
Matthew 6:19-21, KJV

WHERE'S PAW-PAW?

My dog knows Mark as "Paw-Paw." In the evenings, Daisy waits for Paw-Paw to come home from work. When it is almost time for him to come home, I ask, "Daisy, where's Paw-Paw?" Daisy turns in circles and anxiously runs up to the door to greet Paw-Paw. Although he isn't home when we play this game, it's a fun way to play with Daisy. When Paw-Paw finally comes home, Daisy is happy.

Last night, we were having family time together. Mark was helping Krista build a barn out of logs, while I confused Daisy by saying, "Daisy, where's Paw-Paw?" Although Mark was right there with her, she still ran to the door and looked for Paw-Paw to come home.

This reminds me of people who are so determined not to believe in Christ that they run away from the obvious, just to try and find a better answer. They don't realize that there *is* no better answer, and to search for something "better" would stretch our faith even more than if we would only have faith and believe!

I find it much easier to believe that God created the world and designed each individual body to function the way it was intended, than to believe that some "big bang" happened from dense matter and created perfectly designed beings with highly complex and intelligently designed functions in each body part. It takes much greater faith to believe in coincidence than in Godincidence. Sometimes we can be as naïve as my sweet little Daisy — looking for more difficult answers, when the answer is right in front of our eyes. Instead of struggling to have faith, rest in the faithful one!

You will seek me and find me when you seek me with all your heart.
Jeremiah 29:13, NIV

THE SAILBOAT

A few years ago, Mark and I went sailing with some friends. We were inexperienced in sailing and had to rely on the knowledge of our friends. When we were far away and returning to land, the sail didn't blow in the right direction. We were forced to paddle back to land because our battery was dead.

Sometimes life is not smooth sailing and we are forced to make difficult choices. We do not have the power or experience to know how to navigate through these waters. At times, God will allow wind to catch the sail and we can smoothly sail to safety. Other times, we must slowly paddle along, relying upon God's guidance. He will give us wisdom and point us in the right direction, but we must paddle home.

In their hearts humans plan their course, but the LORD establishes their steps.
Proverbs 16:9, NIV

THE PEACOCK

In all his material collections, King Solomon kept several species of peacocks (1 Kings 10:22, KJV). Do you think he realized the similarities between himself and the peacock? Male peacocks display their radiant feathers to female peacocks, called peahens. According to *Animal Diversity Web*, "Peahens choose the peacock with the most eyespots because her chicks will hopefully inherit the male's superior immune system and have a greater chance at survival."[30] Like the peacock, King Solomon tried to impress and show his splendor, but to the wrong women. He took 700 wives and 300 concubines and even built high places for all his foreign wives.

There is a fable that tells of a Blue Jay that tied peacock feathers to its tail and strutted near the peacocks. When they discovered that he was not a peacock, they pecked him and stripped him of the feathers. When he returned to the other Blue Jays, they were annoyed with him and told him, "It is not only fine feathers that make fine birds."[31]

King Solomon also learned this lesson. As punishment, God told King Solomon that He would tear most of the kingdom away from his son. He soon discovered that in all his great projects and great collections, he would be left empty. It was all as chasing after the wind.

I denied myself nothing my eyes desired; I refused my heart no pleasure. My heart took delight in all my labor, and this was the reward for all my toil. Yet when I surveyed all that my hands had done and what I had toiled to achieve, everything was meaningless, a chasing after the wind; nothing was gained under the sun.
Ecclesiastes 2:10-11, NIV

5K TRAINING

My friend Beth and I started a new exercise program. This program was designed to take us from being physically inactive to being able to run a 5k. The program started us out slowly, prompting us to run for only a few seconds at a time with a brisk walk between runs.

When we first began, running only 30 seconds felt like an eternity, but we are now able to run for six whole minutes at a time — with fewer brisk walks in between. If we stay on track, we should be able to run a 5k in just a few weeks.

Sometimes we do our exercise routine on that dreadful piece of equipment we refer to as the "dreadmill," but on a cool fall day like today, we prefer to run at the lake. It's easier to run when we are outdoors because we can use landmarks as focal points and create short goals for ourselves. If we can make it to the park bench 75 feet ahead, then surely we can make it a few feet further to the light pole. Meanwhile, we share laughter and tears as we talk about our families, friends, and jobs.

Much can be learned from our exercise adventures. Beth and I couldn't just get out and run a 5k on a whim. It takes hours of sweat and hard training. We have come home with sore bodies and have, at times, wanted to give up. Sometimes life is like our 5k journey — we have to set small goals and take life one step at a time. Just as Beth and I find a focal point and run toward that mark, the Bible gives us similar advice. "Brothers and sisters, I do not consider myself yet to have taken hold of it. But one thing I do: Forgetting what is behind and straining toward what is ahead, I press on toward the goal to win the prize for which God has called me heavenward in Christ Jesus" (Philippians 3:13-14, NIV).

Each day brings a new adventure and a new challenge. Just as the Israelites had only enough manna for a day at a time, the Lord's prayer says, "Give us this day our daily bread" (Matthew 6:11, KJV). If we ask, God will give us strength for the day. It's always nice to share our journey with a good friend too!

Brothers and sisters, I do not consider myself yet to have taken hold of it. But one thing I do: Forgetting what is behind and straining toward what is ahead, I press on toward the goal to win the prize for which God has called me heavenward in Christ Jesus.
Philippians 3:13-14, NIV

THE PLUM TREE

I have never been able to identify the kind of tree that is planted near the metal shed in my backyard. I tried to figure it out in the winter and again in the early spring, but couldn't identify what type of tree it was. It just looked like an ordinary tree to me. As I walked closer to the tree, I saw a squirrel eating some fruit that had dropped to the ground. I know better than to eat mysterious fruit, but it had to be safe if the squirrel was eating it, right? No, I didn't pick up the fruit and eat it, but Mark did. He finally realized that the mystery tree was a plum tree.

This made me question what kind of fruit I produce. Are people seeing healthy fruit, or fruit that is dry, brown, and stale? Am I alive and flourishing? Ephesians 2:4-5 says, "But because of his great love for us, God, who is rich in mercy, made us alive with Christ even when we were dead in transgressions—it is by grace you have been saved" (NIV).

"No good tree bears bad fruit, nor does a bad tree bear good fruit. Each tree is recognized by its own fruit. People do not pick figs from thornbushes, or grapes from briers. The good man brings good things out of the good stored up in his heart, and an evil man brings evil things out of the evil stored up in his heart. For the mouth speaks what the heart is full of..."
Luke 6:43-45, NIV

THIRSTY BIRDS

After returning from the grocery store, I watched as two birds in my driveway desperately searched for something. I could tell that they were overheated because their mouths were open as if they were panting. I took the groceries inside and intended to bring them a small, shallow dish with cool water. Although I had good intentions, I unloaded the groceries and forgot about my feathered friends. Ten minutes later, a storm approached and a heavy rain pounded the ground. Even though I had forgotten about the birds, God didn't. He knew that the birds were dehydrated and sent a nice rain to cool them off. If God cares this much for the birds in my yard, how much more does He care for us? He doesn't forget us in our times of need. He will bring refreshment to our parched spirits when we need it the most.

Behold the fowls of the air: for they sow not, neither do they reap, nor gather into barns; yet your heavenly Father feedeth them. Are ye not much better than they?
Matthew 6:26, KJV

THE SEARCHLIGHTS

My family was on the way home when we discovered a searchlight moving across the nighttime sky. Krista insisted that we seek out the source of the light. We felt like the wise men following the star that would lead them to baby Jesus.

During World War II, searchlights were used to detect enemy aircraft at night. Today spotlights are used, not to detect, but to attract attention to big events and sales. When we saw the searchlight in the sky, we searched for the source of the light, which was a car dealership.

The Bible tells us in Matthew 5:16, "Let your light so shine before men, that they may see your good works, and glorify your Father which is in heaven" (KJV). Instead of reflecting the light to our Maker, too often we keep the focus on ourselves, unknowingly making ourselves a target for the enemy. We should allow our lights to be a searchlight for those who are searching for the true Light, reflecting the nature of Christ.

Ye are the light of the world. A city that is set on an hill cannot be hid. Neither do men light a candle, and put it under a bushel, but on a candlestick; and it giveth light unto all that are in the house. Let your light so shine before men, that they may see your good works, and glorify your Father which is in heaven.
Matthew 5:14-16, KJV

TOP OF THE TOOLBOX

There are many crazy things that we only see in the South! One thing that we see is dogs riding in the beds of pick-up trucks. Just this week, I was riding through town and saw two hound dogs riding in the back of a truck. The dogs ran from side to side, trying to decide which side of the truck they liked better. When the driver stopped at a red light, one of the dogs bravely jumped on top of the metal toolbox for a real adventure. You would think that the dog's master would have pulled over to make the dog move to a safer place, but he drove the same speed (approximately 45 MPH) and turned onto a sharp, curved incline. The dog just stood still and kept hanging on. He loved the view and the cool air in his face. I just knew there would have to be toenail marks on the toolbox because he was holding on so tightly. I worried that the dog would fall off, but he never did.

Sometimes I feel like I'm a hound dog on top of a tool box. I feel like I'm trying to hold on while life takes me for a wild ride. It's hard to hold on when the ride gets bumpy and adversity is all around. Why in the world was that hound dog on top of the toolbox? It is because he chose to see adventure — not trouble. He had a broader view on top of the toolbox than he had in the bed of the truck. He was also closer to his master, whom he trusted.

When we are in the midst of adversity, we often have a better view of life and begin to appreciate the important things in life — our family and friends, our jobs, and our health. We also tend to cling closer to our heavenly Master in adversity. He is where our hope comes from. James 1:2-4 says, "Consider it pure joy, my brothers and sisters, whenever you face trials of many kinds, because you know that the testing of your faith produces perseverance. Let perseverance finish its work so that you may be mature and complete, not lacking anything" (NIV). So why didn't the master pull over and move the dog to a safer place? While I still don't understand why he would let the dog be in such a dangerous place, I can only come to the conclusion that he knew that his dog would be safe. He also wanted his dog to have a better view. At times, I don't understand why God allows us to go through many of the things that we go through, but we must remember that God has a plan. He knows how much we can handle, and He knows that adversity often makes us grow in faith and become closer to Him. Like the hound dog, we must trust our Master and keep holding on!

Let us hold unswervingly to the hope we profess, for he who promised is faithful.
Hebrews 10:23, NIV

WHO'S BIGGER?

Krista called me to the window to show me a lizard. "Look, mama! The lizard is shaking his head 'yes' at you." The lizard moved its head up and down to show us that it was annoyed by our presence. It expanded its throat to expose a red color and showed us its open mouth. A lizard may push itself up or bob its head to defend its territory by making itself look bigger. It may also expand its throat and open its jaws as a warning sign. God reminded me how people who are insecure may act the same way. Out of fear or pride, they try to build themselves up by bragging on themselves, or by tearing others down.

Years after this incident with the lizard, I was listening to someone brag about himself and the fine things that he owned. I couldn't believe the nerve of this person! I was angry and wanted so badly to tell him what I thought of his behavior. It was as though lightning hit me! Something told me to look over at the fence. There I saw a bright, green lizard blowing its throat out and doing push-ups. Chills ran up my spine as I felt God gently remind me of what he taught me years before. "Don't be upset, Amy!" I felt Him say. The anger quickly vanished and was replaced with a smile.

Greater love hath no man than this, that a man lay down his life for his friends.
John 15:13, KJV

RIGHT ON TIME

I am the mom who is darting out the door five minutes before school starts and just getting my child to school right as the tardy bells rings. Just a few weeks ago, I took Krista to school and promised I'd be there at 11:40 to have lunch with her. I didn't pack her lunch that day because I wanted to surprise her with a special lunch. At 11:45, I rushed through the cafeteria doors — 5 minutes late! Krista was sitting at the table and watching the door while the other kids enjoyed their lunch. As we ate our lunch under a shade tree, I asked Krista if she was worried that I wouldn't show up for lunch. She replied, "Of course not, Mama! I knew you'd come." There was no doubt in her mind that I would be there if I said I would. God reminded me of all the times that I didn't have such faith in Him. There were many times when I didn't trust His timing or believe that He would do as He promised.

Matthew 18:3 says, "And he said: 'Truly I tell you, unless you change and become like little children, you will never enter the kingdom of heaven...'" (NIV). Most children have strong faith in their parents. When they wake up in the morning, they do not have to worry about having milk in the fridge or clean clothes to wear. There is no doubt in their minds that they will be taken care of. While humans are fallible, God is not.

Numbers 23:19 tells us, "God is not human, that he should lie, not a human being, that he should change his mind. Does he speak and then not act? Does he promise and not fulfill?" (NIV). God never fails us! If my child can have unwavering faith in me — a mere human, why can't I have faith in a God who created the universe — a God who never fails! God is never late, but is always right on time. It may not be in the timing we would like, but His timing is perfect. Well, gotta run! School starts in 20 minutes and I still have much to do.

But they that wait upon the Lord shall renew their strength; they shall mount up with wings as eagles; they shall run, and not be weary; and they shall walk, and not faint.
Isaiah 40:31, KJV

TRAVELLER'S ENDURANCE

A few years ago, my parents visited a museum containing historical pieces from the US Civil War. One of my parents' most favorite pieces of history was a picture of Robert E. Lee riding on his horse, "Traveller." While admiring the Civil War art, my mother said that she would love to have a copy of the painting of Robert E. Lee riding his "horse." A gentleman standing beside her corrected her by saying, "That is no horse — that is Traveller."

A horse is a horse, but Traveller was no ordinary horse. This was General Lee's most treasured possession and a horse with his master's vision. Major Thomas L. Brown said, "He needed neither whip nor spur, and would walk his five or six miles an hour over the rough mountain roads of Western Virginia with his rider sitting firmly in the saddle and holding him in check by a tight rein, such vim and eagerness did he manifest to go right ahead so soon as he was mounted."[32]

Traveller was eager and willing to follow his master and surely endured extreme conditions such as hot and cold weather, hunger, thirst, and other dangers along the path. Traveller was not just any horse, but a horse that could teach us about endurance. He was a true "Traveller," traveling miles and enduring both good and bad for the sake of his master.

As Christians, we should be like Traveller — eager and willing to follow our Master's direction, enduring whatever extreme conditions we face.

Thou therefore endure hardness, as a good soldier of Jesus Christ. No man that warreth entangleth himself

with the affairs of this life; that he may please him who hath chosen him to be a soldier.
2 Timothy 2:3-4, KJV

PEANUT BUTTER & ANT SANDWICH

Peanut butter and ant sandwich, anyone? It doesn't sound appealing to me either, but that's almost what I had for dinner. As I opened up a jar of peanut butter from my kitchen pantry, I discovered an army of ants doing backstrokes in my creamy peanut butter. My immediate reaction was to scream and throw the jar of peanut butter down. The jar was screwed on tightly, so I can't figure out how those pesky ants got into my peanut butter. I guess they were just persistent.

Revelation 3:7-8 says, "And to the angel of the church in Philadelphia write; These things saith he that is holy, he that is true, he that hath the key of David, he that openeth, and no many shutteth; and shutteth, and no man openeth; I know thy works: behold, I have set before thee an open door, and no man can shut it: for thou hast a little strength, and hast kept my word, and hast not denied my name" (KJV). Revelation 3:7 teaches us that God is able to close doors. Experience has taught me that closed doors are often blessings from God. Almost every closed door that I've encountered has resulted in God having something better in store.

Like the persistent ants in my pantry that were able to get through the closed jar of peanut butter, God also has the power to open doors that are closed. When Paul and Silas were in prison, they were praying and singing — at midnight! I can imagine that some of the prisoners were probably singing along, while others probably wished they could silence Paul and Silas. Suddenly, there was a great earthquake — "so that the foundations of the prison were shaken: and immediately all the doors were opened, and every one's bands were loosed" (Acts 16:25-26, KJV). Not only were the prison doors opened, but the shackles fell off, and the foundations of the prison were shaken. When God wants a door to be open, it will be opened. I was driving to work this morning when I saw a business sign that said, "GOD CAN." When we think that a door has been shut forever, God can open it. The next time you are discouraged over a closed door, you can rest in knowing that whether God closes a door or opens it, He has your best interest at heart. The next time you open a jar of peanut butter, watch for ants.

> *For with God nothing shall be impossible.*
> Luke 1:37, KJV

THE HOUSE ON THE HILL

My friend Amy and I took our daughters to a fall festival. The girls enjoyed all of the fall activities, but still wanted to go "trick or treating" after the festival ended. It was dark when we left the fall festival, and many of the houses had stopped handing out candy, but we did manage to get some candy from a few houses where the lights were still on. This made the girls very happy. We came to one very large home that was on a steep hill. After climbing what seemed like a thousand steps, we decided that there must be a serious party going on inside. There were several cars outside and Halloween decorations galore. When we approached the door, we could hear people talking and laughing, but they couldn't hear us as we rang the doorbell and knocked.

This reminded me of Jesus' teachings about the narrow door and Heaven. He told a story of someone knocking and pleading for the owner of a house to open the door, but it was too late. The doors had been closed and he could not enter in (Luke 13:22-27). Knock while the light is still burning and salvation is here. You don't want to miss out on the biggest celebration ever.

Then Jesus went through the towns and villages, teaching as he made his way to Jerusalem. Someone asked him, "Lord, are only a few people going to be saved?" He said to them, "Make every effort to enter through the narrow door, because many, I tell you, will try to enter and will not be able to. Once the owner of the house gets up and closes the door, you will stand outside knocking and pleading, 'Sir, open the door for us.' "But he will answer, 'I don't know you or where you come from.' "Then you will say, 'We ate and drank with you, and you taught in our

streets.' "But he will reply, 'I don't know you or where you come from. Away from me, all you evildoers!'…"
Luke 13:22-27, NIV

WHEN THE LIGHTS GO OUT!

This morning I stumbled out of bed. The night owl in me loves to stay up late and sleep in, but I struggle to get out of bed the next morning. As I opened the refrigerator door to look for the milk, a moth flew into the refrigerator. It was attracted to the light, but didn't realize that when the door closed, the light would go out, and it would be dark again.

On the way to work, I heard a song on the radio about the moon and the stars that God created. Some of my favorite times as a child were spent watching the moon in the sky, while riding down the road with my mom and dad. While listening to the song about the nighttime sky, it occurred to me that the moon is nothing more than a giant rock with craters in it — a really cold place with no life. The moon does not shine at all, yet people admire its beauty at night. The light it gives is not its own light, but merely a reflection of the sun. Like my refrigerator, the moon shows light, but it is really just a dark and lonely place.

God gently revealed to me that I am beautiful to Him because He created me, but I am more beautiful to Him and others when I reflect the light of the Son and people see Jesus in me!

When Jesus spoke again to the people, he said, "I am the light of the world. Whoever follows me will never walk in darkness, but will have the light of life."
John 8:12, NIV

A TOUCH OF HIS FEATHERS

For the past two nights, I haven't slept well due to some health concerns. Although I feel better and am fairly certain that the problem is minor, I made an appointment with my physician.

On the second restless night, fear consumed me. Lying in the darkness, I reached my hands toward the sky praying, "Jesus, Great Physician, please touch me and comfort me. Hold me in your hands and allow me to rest in your presence." I longed to feel His touch, but I knew that a physical touch was unlikely.

The next morning while attending Bible study with my closest sisters in Christ, we read Psalm 91:4, which was about God's faithfulness. The word "feather" stuck out in my mind, but I didn't realize that this verse was meant for me. Later that evening, I picked up my Bible, unprepared as to what I would read. My Bible opened to the book of Psalms — one of my favorite books. Astoundingly, the first verse that I read was the same as earlier that day, "He will cover you with his feathers, and under his wings you will find refuge; his faithfulness will be your shield and rampart. You will not fear the terror of night, nor the arrow that flies by day..." (Psalm 91:4-5, NIV).

God wanted me to know that He was listening to me that night as I longed so desperately for His touch. He covered me with His feathers and gave me refuge under His wings. With God's feathers covering me, I do not have to fear the terror of night. When you desperately seek a touch from the Master, He may be standing behind you with His hand on your shoulder.

He will cover you with his feathers, and under his wings you will find refuge; his faithfulness will be your shield and rampart. You will not fear the terror of night, nor the

arrow that flies by day, nor the pestilence that stalks in the darkness, nor the plague that destroys at midday.
Psalm 91:4-6, NIV

THE STOOL

Nobody puts Daddy on a stool! For years, my dad has played music. It's what he lives for, and nothing makes him happier. He taught his children to play different instruments when we were younger, but he refused to let us learn to play an instrument while sitting down. His reason was if we learned to play sitting down, we would never be able to play standing up.

This weekend, our family had to play music at a little church that I grew up in. My dad wasn't feeling his best that night. When he got out his banjo to play, a younger gentleman thought that my dad seemed weak and followed him around — trying to get him to sit down on a stool. My dad wanted nothing to do with that stool! It was funny to watch him avoid the stool. He would step forward, and the man would move the stool forward. He would step backward, and the man would move the stool backward. Finally, with the stool in the way of his microphone, dad moved forward and sang right over the stool, but he refused to sit down.

You're probably thinking, *Can there really be a lesson in this story?* More than you can know! Keep standing — even when you are feeling weak and weary!

Like my daddy, Moses wouldn't allow the Israelites to sit down either. He refused to train up these people the wrong way. If they got used to sitting when they were weak and weary, they would never make it to the Promised Land. While being chased by Pharaoh and his army, the Israelites started to doubt. Moses said, "Do not be afraid. Stand firm and you will see the deliverance the LORD will bring you today. The Egyptians you see today you will never see again. The LORD will fight for you; you need only to be still" (Exodus 14:13-14, NIV).

Stand firm then, with the belt of truth buckled around your waist, with the breastplate of righteousness in place...
Ephesians 6:14, NIV

THE WINDOW
THAT WASN'T THERE

Krista and I were out shopping when we saw a blind man stumbling across the road. He obviously wasn't used to his blindness because he appeared to be struggling with the white stick he carried as he stumbled across the roads and curbs. His friend helped him cross the street by holding onto his arm and directing his steps. Krista asked if it would be worse to be blind, or to be deaf. I told her that it would definitely be worse to be blind. There is always sign language for the deaf, but it would be hard to get along in life without vision.

A few years ago, my dad was given a rather unusual assignment. He paints homes and businesses by profession, but this time he was given a more challenging assignment — to paint a window in the basement of the courthouse. What you probably don't realize is that there *was* no window in the basement. Instead, he was challenged to use his artistic ability to create a new atmosphere. What was once a dark and lonely room was transformed into a room overlooking a beautiful, snow-covered mountain with fall-colored trees.

Proverbs 29:18 says, "Where there is no vision, the people perish: but he that keepeth the law, happy is he" (KJV). While this verse may refer to those who do not know Christ, it can be a great reminder to us all. Just like the basement of the courthouse, we often see life as a dark and dreary place and think that things will not get any better. Our circumstances may or may not change, but isn't it better to think positively and hope for the best? If there is no brightness outside, paint a pretty picture and see the good things in our lives. Remember, all the great artists had to have a vision for the scene they wanted to create before they brushed across the canvas.

Finally, brethren, whatsoever things are true, whatsoever things are honest, whatsoever things are just, whatsoever things are pure, whatsoever things are lovely, whatsoever things are of good report; if there be any virtue, and if there be any praise, think on these things.
Philippians 4:8, KJV

TUNED IN

When you hear the croaking of frogs at night, do you wonder what they are saying? It is believed that certain species of frogs have ears that are only tuned to hear the call of a similar frequency, which narrows down the search for a mate. *Welcomewildlife.com* reports, "In 2008, scientists discovered a species of frogs living near a noisy area in China who can tune their hearing to different frequencies, like a radio knob, effectively tuning out objectionable noises or even the calls of other frog species."[33]

In the Bible, Samuel was tuned to hearing God's voice, but he didn't realize that it was God calling him. After Samuel heard the voice three times, Eli told Samuel that he should tell the Lord to "Speak, LORD, for your servant is listening" (1 Samuel 3:10, NIV).

We are blessed that God speaks to us through his Spirit. Sometimes we don't recognize that it is God speaking, but He makes Himself known to us through His Word, circumstances, nature, etc. Sometimes He even repeats what He wants us to hear. When He calls, we should say, "Speak, LORD, for your servant is listening."

The LORD came and stood there, calling as at the other times, "Samuel! Samuel!" Then Samuel said, "Speak, for your servant is listening."
1 Samuel 3:10, NIV

DAISY'S SURGERY

It was a rough day for my dog. She has had a bladder infection for a couple of weeks. After antibiotics didn't resolve the problem, the vet performed an emergency surgery to remove bladder stones the size of marbles. Daisy whined and whimpered as I drove her home. She was in an enormous amount of pain, and so was I. My heart ached for my furry baby to feel better. Had I made a huge mistake? Without the surgery, she would not have healed. I hope that Daisy understood that I did this to give her a better future — not to harm her. At that time, Jeremiah 29:11 made perfect sense! "For I know the plans I have for you," declares the LORD, "plans to prosper you and not to harm you, plans to give you a hope and a future" (NIV).

God doesn't have the limited vision that we have. We may not understand why things are as they are. Like Daisy, we may only know that we are hurting, but God sees the big picture. He knows the present, past, and future.

Revelation 1:8 says, "I am Alpha and Omega, the beginning and the ending, saith the Lord, which is, and which was, and which is to come, the Almighty" (KJV). Something good has already come from this painful event — I have been taught a great lesson. What we don't understand this side of Heaven, we will surely understand one day.

For my thoughts are not your thoughts, neither are your ways my ways, saith the LORD. For as the heavens are higher than the earth, so are my ways higher than your ways, and my thoughts than your thoughts.
Isaiah 55:8-9, KJV

SEEDS OF DOUBT

For Valentine's Day, Mark gave me a strawberry growing kit, complete with a pot and seeds. I wanted this kit for quite some time and was eager to watch my new plant grow. When I opened the seed packet, there were only a few tiny strawberry seeds. I planted the seeds, but had no faith that my strawberry plant would grow because of the size and amount of the seeds.

As expected, the seeds never sprouted — not because of their size, but because of my lack of faith. I had already decided that it was impossible for the seeds to ever become a plant because of their tiny size and number. Therefore, I neglected to water the seeds regularly. Without water, the plant never grew.

Jesus said in Matthew 17:20-21, "If ye have faith as a grain of mustard seed, ye shall say unto this mountain, Remove hence to yonder place; and it shall remove; and nothing shall be impossible unto you" (KJV). In Matthew 13:32 (NIV), we are told that the tiny mustard seed produces one of the largest garden plants and becomes a tree that the birds perch on. Are you facing a problem that seems too large? Remember that God can do great things, but you must know that your faith in God is greater than the problems you encounter. As we water the seeds of faith daily in God's promises, our faith grows.

And Jesus said unto them, Because of your unbelief: for verily I say unto you, If ye have faith as a grain of mustard seed, ye shall say unto this mountain, Remove hence to yonder place; and it shall remove; and nothing shall be impossible unto you. Howbeit this kind goeth not out but by prayer and fasting.
Matthew 17:20-21, KJV

LOST DOG

I went to visit my friend Beth, who recently downsized into a smaller home. Her new home is located in the city and is convenient for shopping and our favorite hangout that serves iced lattes. She was telling me a story about her dog, Roxie. Roxie is 14-years-old and has to take daily shots for diabetes. She also suffers from arthritis in her feet, so she is usually resting when I visit. Beth told me a story about how Roxie got lost in the new neighborhood and how she and her husband spent hours searching for Roxie. After searching tirelessly, they posted "Lost Dog" signs around the neighborhood and local shops.

They were awakened at 1:30 AM by a neighbor who called to report that she had seen Roxie. Beth didn't wait until morning. Instead, she and her husband jumped in the car and went to find Roxie. When they made it to the neighbor's house, the neighbor warned that Roxie had wandered down near a lake where alligators had been seen at times. Beth rushed down the dark path to rescue her beloved Roxie. At first she didn't see Roxie, but then turned around and discovered her lying on the ground. Beth's reaction when she saw Roxie — "I snatched that 65-pound dog up just like she was nothing!" She was so happy to see Roxie that she went into the dark of night to find her. Despite Roxie's size, Beth lifted her just like she was her child. Matthew 12:11-12 tells a story about Jesus healing a man with a withered hand on the Sabbath. When accused, he told them, "What man shall there be among you, that shall have one sheep, and if it fall into a pit on the sabbath day, will he not lay hold on it, and lift it out? How much then is a man better than a sheep?..." (KJV)

We are no different than Roxie. We have all gone astray, or needed rescuing at some point. God is able to come to our rescue. He is able to help us spiritually and physically. He can lift us out of sin, depression, loneliness, addictions, and even sickness! As Beth loves Roxie, God loves us and is able to snatch us up and take us to safety.

Even the youths shall faint and be weary, and the young men shall utterly fall: But they that wait upon the LORD shall renew their strength; they shall mount up with wings as eagles; they shall run, and not be weary; and they shall walk, and not faint.
Isaiah 40:30-31, KJV

THE STRINGS CONCERT

I recently attended a strings concert featuring young musicians in our school system. I enjoyed watching the talented, young musicians perform the songs they had spent hours practicing. The music instructors and parents beamed with pride as the youngsters performed. I am proud to have such an incredible program in our community.

While the music performed at this concert was beautiful and expressed many different emotions, I must admit that my favorite part of an orchestra concert is the tuning of the stringed instruments. I just love the sound of all the bows sliding across the strings of the violins and cellos as they all tune to the same note. On this particular evening, I watched as the nervous and excited young musicians tuned their instruments together to perfect harmony. This was a small strings concert, but oboes are often used in large orchestras as the main instrument to which all other instruments tune. *Wikipedia* states, "According to the League of American Orchestras, 'this is done because the pitch of the oboe is secure and its penetrating sound makes it ideal for tuning purposes.'"[34]

An instrument can easily get out of tune with any changes in temperature or humidity, so the performers tune before the concert begins to ensure that they are in perfect harmony.

I think of the tuning of the instruments and how Christians are like an orchestra. Although we all have different personalities, backgrounds, and abilities, we all have the same purpose — to glorify God. Like the oboe, God has a unique voice. Sometimes we struggle to hear God's voice, but His voice can be heard if we will listen carefully. John 10:27-28 tells us, "My sheep hear my voice, and I know them, and they follow me: And I give unto them eternal life; and they shall never perish, neither shall any man pluck them out of my hand" (KJV). Let us listen carefully for His voice and be in perfect tune with Him!

My sheep hear my voice, and I know them, and they follow me: And I give unto them eternal life; and they shall never perish, neither shall any man pluck them out of my hand.
John 10:27-28, KJV

THE DEAD BATTERY

On several occasions, I have walked to my car after work to discover a dead battery. I have a long drive to work and often have to use my headlights to see through thick fog and rain. The fog usually clears and the sun shines brightly by the time I arrive at work, which causes me to forget to turn off my headlights. I don't realize that my headlights are still on when the sun is shining and the weather is fair, but when I return to my car and discover a dead battery, I suddenly remember what I forgot to do. The headlights drain the battery of its energy and there is no power left to start the car.

This reminds me of our spiritual lives. We are often so busy that we feel just as drained as this battery. We work, take care of our families, entertain in our homes, volunteer, and enjoy our hobbies. We think everything is going just fine, but at the end of the day, we are so drained of energy that we have nothing left. Like the dead battery, we can even feel drained – spiritually that is!

Many people believe that God wants us to be constantly busy. Although He has plans for us and wants us to enjoy life, He also wants us to rest and enjoy Him! Matthew 11:28-30 says, "Come unto me, all ye that labour and are heavy laden, and I will give you rest. Take my yoke upon you, and learn of me; for I am meek and lowly in heart: and ye shall find rest unto your souls. For my yoke is easy, and my burden is light" (KJV). He doesn't mean for us to stop everything we are doing, but to slow down, make time for Him, and rest in Him.

I am thankful for the gentleman in our office who used his battery cables to jump-start my car. Let God be the spark that brings life to our hearts too.

He giveth power to the faint; and to them that have no might he increaseth strength. Even the youths shall faint and be weary, and the young men shall utterly fall: But they that wait upon the LORD shall renew their strength; they shall mount up with wings as eagles; they shall run, and not be weary; and they shall walk, and not faint.
Isaiah 40:29-31, KJV

THE ANIMAL-PRINT SWEATER

I am wearing my favorite sweater on this cold winter day. There are many reasons why this is my favorite sweater. It is probably the warmest sweater that I have, and the neutral colors match almost every black outfit that I wear. I also love this sweater because of the story behind it.

My family was living in South Florida when I became sick. Mark accepted a job offer, but I was too sick to ride in a bumpy moving van. He packed our belongings, while Krista and I flew back on a plane.

South Florida is warm almost year round, so when we arrived at the airport in Tallahassee, I didn't have a jacket with me and it was freezing outside! I was pleasantly surprised when my mom met me at the terminal with a tan and black animal print sweater in her hand. She knew that I wouldn't be prepared for the extreme drop in temperature, so she stopped at the thrift shop and purchased the sweater for a dollar. It has been the best dollar she ever spent! I receive compliments every time I wear my sweater.

This sweater reminds me of the story of the prodigal son. In this story, the son was living far away from home. His father had given him a share of his estate, and the son went to a distant land and squandered the money away in wild living. After spending all of the money, the son took a job feeding pigs and was so hungry that he longed to eat the food that the pigs were eating. He decided to return home and beg for his father's forgiveness. The father ran to his son, threw his arms around him, and kissed him. Then he sent his servants to bring his best robe for the boy to wear, a ring for his finger, and sandals for his feet. His father met him with a robe —

almost like my mom met me with the sweater (Luke 15:11-31).

Like the father in this story, our Father has clothed us. When Adam and Eve sinned in the Garden, God made clothes for them out of animal skin. Where did He get the animal skin? There was no faux fur in that day, so an animal obviously had to die! My animal print sweater reminds me of how God covers me with salvation through the sacrifice of His Son. Isaiah 61:10 says, "I will greatly rejoice in the LORD, my soul shall be joyful in my God; for he hath clothed me with the garments of salvation, he hath covered me with the robe of righteousness, as a bridegroom decketh himself with ornaments, and as a bride adorneth herself with her jewels" (KJV). We are never so far away that God will not welcome us home!

And the Spirit and the bride say, Come. And let him that heareth say, Come. And let him that is athirst come. And whosoever will, let him take the water of life freely.
Revelation 22:17, KJV

PAID IN FULL

I was looking through an old book when I discovered a receipt folded between the pages. The receipt from 1980, addressed to Miss Shirley in the amount of $109, was for rent that she paid on her mobile home. Miss Shirley was a friend of our family, who was born with Down's Syndrome. Although Miss Shirley was physically handicapped, she was extremely talented! She wrote beautiful poetry and even played the piano with only three fingers on each hand. I always watched in awe as she played her favorite song, "Whispering Hope." I looked forward to an occasional Friday night when Miss Shirley would come over and sit with me while my parents enjoyed a date night. We had pizza together and watched our favorite Friday night television shows.

When I found the receipt stuck between the pages of the old book, I thought $109 seemed really inexpensive for rent. In reality, it probably seemed like a fortune for Miss Shirley because she was on a limited income. At the bottom of the receipt was a line that caught my attention: "Rent must be paid in advance!" I wondered what would have happened if Miss Shirley missed that rent payment. Surely they wouldn't have evicted her; she was such a good person. Who could not love Miss Shirley? Nothing in life is free though, so maybe they would have evicted her. Thankfully, the payment was made, and she lived many years in that mobile home.

Jesus had finished business too! The last words spoken of our Savior on the cross were, "It is finished!" which was a translation of the Greek term, "Tetelestai." *Hardwire Ministries (Men of Destiny)* explains, "Commercially, the word tetelestai was an accounting term. It was stamped on a receipt when a debt had been paid in full. It meant that the payment-obligation had come to an end; it had been perfected and rendered complete."[35]

Like Miss Shirley, we may be considered "good" or "loveable," but without the blood of Christ covering our sins, the Bible says our righteousness is as filthy rags (Isaiah 64:5, KJV). When Jesus uttered the precious words, "It is finished..." (John 19:30, KJV), He paid our debt of sin in full. We must only accept that gift.

Miss Shirley has since passed away and I think of her often. She no longer has to pay rent because, thanks to Jesus' payment on the cross, she has a place of her own.

Let not your heart be troubled: ye believe in God, believe also in me. In my Father's house are many mansions: if it were not so, I would have told you. I go to prepare a place for you. And if I go and prepare a place for you, I will come again, and receive you unto myself; that where I am, there ye may be also.
John 14:1-3, KJV

THE BLACK SWAN

My friend Suzanne retired and is now enjoying time with her children and grandchildren. One of her favorite activities is going to the park to feed the ducks. Last year, she received a nasty bruise after being attacked by a cautious swan, but that doesn't stop Suzanne from visiting the park and feeding the ducks. She recently spent an afternoon at the park with her daughter Stacey, and they took a veggie sub sandwich to share for lunch. As they sat on some steps and enjoyed their sandwich, a black swan waddled up to see what they were eating. They laughed at the silly-looking swan with straw and animal waste hanging from its beak. Yuck! When Stacey pulled out her camera to snap a picture of the curious swan, it waddled away. Suzanne was about to take a bite of her sub sandwich, when the swan leaned over her shoulder to take a bite too. This scared Suzanne and, remembering the attack swan from last year, she jumped up and left the sandwich for the hungry swan's lunch.

While I can't say that I blame her for running, this reminded me of how things from the past can keep us from a good future. Past failures and hurtful relationships can keep us from what God may have in store for us. Satan naturally doesn't want us to succeed, be happy, or do the things that God has for us to do, so he is always willing to bring up reminders of our past. He also uses fear of the unknown future to keep us from moving forward to the place God has for us. 2 Timothy 1:7 says, "For God hath not given us the spirit of fear; but of power, and of love, and of a sound mind" (KJV).

When the Israelites sent twelve spies into Canaan to investigate the land, the spies came back reporting that Canaan was, indeed, a good place with rich land. They brought back a single cluster of grapes so large that it had to be carried between two poles!

Ten of the spies reported that although Canaan would be a good place to settle, there were giants in the land, and the Israelites surely wouldn't be able to defeat them. They compared themselves to grasshoppers next to these giants. You see, they had already lost — *in their minds!* God had already delivered them from Egypt, but this was a new problem and one that seemed insurmountable. What happened to these spies? While they could have easily defeated the giants with the help of God, they instead died by plague before the Lord (Numbers 14:37, NIV).

Don't be afraid to face your fears. Like the black swan, Satan is ready to take away our blessings. Will we give in or put up a fight?

Be strong and of a good courage, fear not, nor be afraid of them: for the LORD thy God, he it is that doth go with thee; he will not fail thee, nor forsake thee.
Deuteronomy 31:6, KJV

THE CALCULATOR

I am thankful to God for allowing me to be called a "saint," although I certainly don't feel like one at times. After this story, you may feel the same way about me. I had a job interview for a part-time position and expected for the interview to be a piece-of-cake experience. I have interviewed for several jobs throughout my life, and most of the interviews have been great experiences. The job interview that I had today was not one of those experiences. I wasn't prepared and had a difficult time answering the questions that were asked. The more serious problem was the math test I had to take. I am a writer — NOT a mathematician! To be honest, I really don't like numbers. I currently work in a job which requires good math skills. The difference is that I use a calculator in my job and don't have to figure the totals in my mind.

While on the job interview today, I sat for quite some time figuring the formulas in my mind, but I struggled with not being able to see the formulas in front of my eyes. After some time had passed, I reached into my pocket, pulled out my mobile phone, and used the calculator tool to find the answer. I know it was probably not the best thing to do, but I had already decided that I didn't want the job — even if it was offered to me, so I had nothing to lose.

I have personally faced many difficult decisions lately. Decisions are particularly hard for me — especially when I want to follow God's will for my life. Like the math test, sometimes life seems unclear, and we don't know the answers to our problems. We have limited vision and struggle to find the answers that we need. God is like my calculator — always there to help me figure out a solution to my daily dilemmas. When things don't add up, run to the one who has the answers!

A man's heart deviseth his way: but the Lord directeth his steps.
Proverbs 16:9, KJV

THE SISTINE CHAPEL

I watched as Krista and her grandma, whom she calls "Dannaw," had their special touch. Dannaw sticks out her index finger, and Krista meets it with her own little index finger. It is their own special way of saying, "I see you and I love you!" Years from now, this may be Krista's way of expressing love to her own grandchild.

I was riding through the country today when I saw a similar image of two fingers reaching for each other. The church sign bore an image of the famous painting called *The Creation of Adam*, by Michelangelo.

The Creation of Adam was one of the paintings on the Sistine Chapel ceiling. Michelangelo was a sculptor and wasn't thrilled when Pope Julius II gave him the massive artistic assignment. *EyeWitnesstoHistory.com* explains, "Michelangelo at first refused, protesting that he was a sculptor, not a painter. However, Pope Julius insisted and finally prevailed. It was arduous work that required the artist to constantly paint while lying on his back atop a scaffold that raised him to within inches of the ceiling. However, Michelangelo not only overcame these obstacles, but after four years, revealed a masterpiece."[36] These paintings would leave people awestruck for years to come.

Many think that *The Creation of Adam* depicts God giving life to Adam by reaching to touch his finger. While no one knows the true intention of this painting, it reminds me of Krista and Dannaw's intimate touch — their way of saying, "I see you and I love you!"

God is always reaching for us like Dannaw reaches for Krista, and like *The Creation of Adam* painting. Every day, we can see the beauty that He has made, and it tells of His love for us. Like the huge Sistine Chapel ceiling, God paints his own incredible scenes for our enjoyment and His glory. Look at the wind-swept clouds in the skies, and see the colorful red and yellow highlights on the trees in the fall season. There may be a Yellow Finch perched in the branches of a tree outside your kitchen window. It's as though God has a paintbrush and creates a beautiful scene for us to enjoy. He is saying, "I see you and I love you!"

When I consider thy heavens, the work of thy fingers, the moon and the stars, which thou hast ordained; What is man, that thou art mindful of him? and the son of man, that thou visitest him?
Psalm 8:3-4, KJV

THE MOVIE THEATER

My friend Suzanne and her daughter Stacey enjoy hanging out together. One of their favorite places to hang out is the movies. Suzanne tells a story of a time when she and Stacey went to see a movie that they had been waiting to see. The movie theater was already dark and the movie was about to begin, so they stumbled through the darkness to find their seats, and they sat down together — on the laps of a man and his date! Suzanne and Stacey jumped up quickly and moved to a vacant seat, but couldn't stop laughing throughout the whole movie.

It's hard to see in a dark room — especially when you are used to being outside on a sunny day before entering the darkness. Isaiah 59:9-10 says, "Therefore is judgment far from us, neither doth justice overtake us: we wait for light, but behold obscurity; for brightness, but we walk in darkness. We grope for the wall like the blind, and we grope as if we had no eyes: we stumble at noon day as in the night; we are in desolate places as dead men" (KJV). This verse talks about how sin can keep us in the dark.

Without God's light, we stumble through life and don't know where we are going, or what we are doing. We sometimes even wonder what the purpose of life is. We don't know how to get through troubles or obstacles and have no hope whatsoever. Our hearts long for something that we can't fill.

Many times at night, I will wake up in the darkness and feel for the door. Why? Because I have hit my head on that door so many times that I know to look out for it. This is how the blind get along in life — by feeling their way around. I don't simply want to go by feeling; I'd rather go by knowing. The next time you see a movie, be careful where you sit!

Then spake Jesus again unto them, saying, I am the light of the world: he that followeth me shall not walk in darkness, but shall have the light of life.
John 8:12, KJV

THE RED BANDANA

At the beginning of the summer, Krista and I took a day trip to the beach. School was out, and we longed to feel the warm sun. We collected shells, played in the sand, and watched the planes draw lines in the sky. After a few hours, we started the long drive home. We were sharing stories on the way home when I suddenly slammed on the brakes and nearly rear-ended a truck that was hauling a boat in the truck bed. What caught my attention and saved me from a near catastrophe was a simple red bandana tied onto the end of the protruding boat. I am certain that I would have collided with the vehicle if I had not seen the red bandana waving in the wind.

In John 1:23, the priests and Levites were questioning John when he replied, "I am the voice of one calling in the wilderness, 'Make straight the way for the Lord'" (NIV). John captured the attention of many people, but placed all the focus on Jesus. Further in the chapter, John described how he had seen the Spirit come down from Heaven and remain on Jesus. John saw Jesus as God's chosen and revealed that to everyone he saw. John was like the red bandana that drew attention to the boat. Instead, he drew attention to the Son of God.

On the day that I saw the red bandana flapping in the wind, I felt God calling me to be a red bandana. I believe that He calls us all to be red bandanas and tell others about Him. He is a real, living God and wants us to have a relationship with Him and see Him in everything. Unfortunately, many don't see Him — just as I didn't see the boat. We can see Him in everything we look at. He made the sky and everything in it. He made the trees that stand with their branches outstretched to praise Him. He made the sunflower that turns its head to follow the sun. Everything out there seems to worship the living God, so why don't we? In writing this, I am making an effort to be that red bandana, and I hope that throughout your day, you will see the Living God and will also be a red bandana to someone.

There was a man sent from God, whose name was John. The same came for a witness, to bear witness of the Light, that all men through him might believe. He was not that Light, but was sent to bear witness of that Light.
John 1:6-8, KJV

THE "LOSS PREVENTION" OFFICER

I recently bought a pair of painful shoes at a department store. Rather than keep the shoes and never wear them, I returned them to the department store for a refund. As I came in the door, I noticed a gentleman who was directing me to the "Returns" line. I originally just thought that he was a friendly greeter, but later saw that he was wearing a "Loss Prevention" vest over his shirt. *Loss prevention — what a politically correct way to say "Security,"* I thought. It was almost as if the store was trying to give this title as a way to disguise what he really was — a security guard! With a title like "Loss Prevention," the people might be tricked into thinking he was simply there to help people to the registers, while he was actually there to prevent merchandise from being stolen. There was obviously reason to believe that a guard was needed. Perhaps merchandise has been stolen before.

    I immediately thought of the guards who watched the tomb of Jesus. The Pharisees and Chief Priests knew who Jesus claimed to be and that He said He would rise again after three days. Like the department store, they set up a "Loss Prevention" plan. They asked Pilate for some guards to watch the tomb so that the disciples would not steal Jesus' body away and make the people think that Jesus had risen from the dead. A large stone was rolled in front of the tomb to ensure that Jesus couldn't be moved. Guards were also put in place to make sure that the tomb's occupant remained there. Like the department store, these leaders wanted what was there to stay there. They were not simply trying to protect the people from being misled. Alas, an angel appeared and rolled the stone away! The angel told the women at the tomb that Jesus had risen.

The "Loss Prevention" officers at the tomb certainly couldn't prevent our Savior from rising from the dead. After this, the leaders paid the guards money to say that the disciples had stolen Jesus' body while the guards slept. (Matthew 28:12). I would love to have seen the front page story on the newspaper that day, if there had been one. What would it have read? I personally would like "RISEN!" but I'm thinking there would have been a more politically correct headline. Perhaps it would have read, "MISPLACED!" I'm happy to know that Jesus wasn't misplaced, but is risen and alive today. As a result, He rescued us from a great loss — of a life with Him!

And as they were afraid, and bowed down their faces to the earth, they said unto them, Why seek ye the living among the dead? He is not here, but is risen: remember how he spake unto you when he was yet in Galilee, Saying, The Son of man must be delivered into the hands of sinful men, and be crucified, and the third day rise again.
Luke 24:5-7, KJV

THE SNAIL

I truly believe that God's mercies are new every morning. Krista and I were out for a ride when she discovered a snail hanging on the side-view mirror for dear life. As I drove faster, the snail released a large amount of sticky slime and clung to the mirror as tightly as it could. I saw the wind tugging at the snail's shell and knew that the wind was more than it could take, so I pulled over to release the weary traveler onto a patch of grass.

This little snail taught me a great lesson about persevering in trouble. When the winds are raging, we need to be like this little snail and hold on for dear life. Hebrews 10:23 says, "Let us hold unswervingly to the hope we profess, for he who promised is faithful" (NIV). This verse gives no indication that life will be an easy ride, but does promise that God will be faithful to us and will give us what we need to endure the journey. If we hold on to our hope, He will be there for us until the winds die down.

Let us hold unswervingly to the hope we profess, for he who promised is faithful.
Hebrews 10:23, NIV

SKYSCRAPER

I sat in my car at work and watched nervously as two men worked on top of a tall building nearby. This building is 19-stories tall and towers high above many other buildings in the city. It is certainly not the highest building ever constructed, but high enough that I wouldn't dare go on the rooftop! These men must be adventurous and have no fear whatsoever to be working at such extreme heights.

In 1932, a photo called *Lunch atop a Skyscraper* was captured and printed in the newspaper. This photograph was taken during construction of the RCA Building at Rockefeller Center in New York City. It is a photo of eleven men having lunch together, but instead of dining in their favorite restaurant, they casually dined together on a girder, hundreds of feet in the air. The photograph shows the men talking, eating, and smoking together, while their feet dangled from the edge of the girder. There was no expression of fear on their faces whatsoever!

What makes some people fearful of heights, while others appreciate the adventure? It is probably not the fear of being up high that makes people afraid, but the fear of falling below. We don't just fear this in heights, but in everything we encounter in life. "What if I fail?" or "What if this doesn't work out?" "What will they think of me?" 2 Timothy 1:7 says, "For God hath not given us the spirit of fear; but of power, and of love, and of a sound mind" (KJV). Does He want us to live recklessly? No, but He also doesn't want us to live a life of fear, what-ifs, or what-if-nots. Fear will often keep us from God's will for our lives, and that is exactly what we do not want. Be like the men on the rooftop — ready and willing to do the work we are called to do, and not afraid of the what-ifs!

Are not two sparrows sold for a penny? Yet not one of them will fall to the ground outside your Father's care.
Matthew 10:29, NIV

CANARY IN A COAL MINE

"I tawt I taw a Puddy Tat!" were the famous words spoken by Tweety Bird in the Looney Tunes show that I watched when I was young.[37] How could anyone not love this cute, yellow canary? Sylvester the "puddy tat" was always after Tweety, but Tweety was always rescued by Granny or Hector, the bulldog. Tweety always came out alive and well.

Not so in the days of the early coal miners. These miners often took yellow canaries into the dangerous mines to determine if toxic gases were present. Canaries were more sensitive to the gases than the miners were and would show distress if toxic gases were encountered. If the canary died, the miners would be aware of the danger and have an opportunity to escape the dangerous mine.

Matthew 24 is our warning system for what Jesus says is coming. It tells how there will be wars, earthquakes, famines, pestilences, false prophets, and many more troubles in the last days. We see these things happening today. There is some good news though. Like the miners, we have an escape at the end of this life. Through Jesus' death on the cross, we are promised eternal life. We don't have to be afraid of what tomorrow holds because we know who holds tomorrow!

These things I have spoken unto you, that in me ye might have peace. In the world ye shall have tribulation: but be of good cheer; I have overcome the world.
John 16:33, KJV

HIGHER AND HIGHER STILL

This summer, Krista and I went on a trip with my parents to the Great Smoky Mountains. While in the mountains, we drove on some narrow and winding roads. Passing another car was not an option on many of the roads, and parking on the side of the road could result in your car rolling off a mountain. Every few miles, there were paved areas where motorists could pull over to rest and see a breathtaking view of the mountains, valleys, and my personal favorite — the smoke rising up off the mountains. It was a sight to behold and truly showed the majesty of the Lord!

We could even look down and see some of the roads that we had traveled on the way up. The one thing I noticed while on this trip was that even when it seemed like we were on the highest mountain, there was always another mountain that was higher. Many times, we were in an elevated valley, but it looked like we were on the highest mountain. Remember this in life — when trials come and everything seems to be going wrong, God has given us a little area where we can pull over and rest in him.

Psalm 62:1-2 says, "Truly my soul finds rest in God; my salvation comes from him. Truly he is my rock and my salvation; he is my fortress, I will never be shaken" (NIV). We can see something spectacular if we take the opportunity. God will show us all the lower valleys He has traveled with us before and the promises He has for our lives. How majestic is the Lord!

In the midst of trials, if we stand firm on the Word of God and fix our eyes on Jesus, we don't have to fear what lies ahead, for *He* is our mountain-top experience! Remember, you can have a mountain-top experience, even when you're not on the highest mountain.

For the Lord is the great God, the great King above all gods. In his hand are the depths of the earth, and the mountain peaks belong to him. The sea is his, for he made it, and his hands formed the dry land.
Psalm 95:3-5, NIV

THE KITTY-CUDDLERS

My friend Suzanne is enjoying her retirement. She exercises at the health club and volunteers weekly at the local humane society. She has even given herself the job title "Kitty Cuddler" to describe the duties that her new volunteer position entails. She doesn't just come in to care for the cats, but also convinces the visitors that the cats would be good companions. Many cats have found new homes because of Suzanne. Suzanne's young granddaughter Katie came to visit with her grandma last week and volunteered at the shelter for the first time. Katie fell in love with the cats and enjoyed cuddling with them.

Many of the animals at the shelter are strays or abandoned pets. Because their names are unknown, the shelter employees give the animals new names to match their personalities and appearances. You can imagine Katie's excitement when the shelter employees allowed her to name three of the cats. She named one cat Katie (after herself), and the other two cats were named Judy and Gracie! The cats found loving homes a day or two later, and this made Katie very happy.

This precious story reminds me of how God adopts us into His family and gives us a new name. In the Bible, Simon was an apostle who I can relate to. He loved Jesus with all his heart, but struggled with living out what he believed. According to *Wikipedia*, "Simon is a common name, from Hebrew meaning 'He who has heard/hears [the word of God].'"[38] Jesus changed Simon's name to Cephas or Peter, meaning "stone" or "rock." Simon Peter not only heard about Jesus as his original name meant, but he believed and was adopted into God's family through faith in Jesus. Jesus knew that Peter would be the "rock" upon which His church would be built.

Like Katie's cats and Peter, God wants to adopt us into His family and give us new names too. Ephesians 1:5-6 tells us about our adoption through Christ — "Having predestinated us unto the adoption of children by Jesus Christ to himself, according to the good pleasure of his will, To the praise of the glory of his grace, wherein he hath made us accepted in the beloved" (KJV). Like Peter, when we go from hearing to believing, God adopts us into His family and gives us a new name. We share in His name when we are called "Christians." This name is not to be taken lightly. To be a Christian is to be a "Christ-follower." That doesn't mean simply going to church or believing in God, but following Jesus daily.

But as many as received him, to them gave he power to become the sons of God, even to them that believe on his name: Which were born, not of blood, nor of the will of the flesh, nor of the will of man, but of God.
John 1:12-13, KJV

LOST GUITAR PICKS

Guitar picks are so much fun! They come in a variety of shapes, colors, and sizes. There are different picks for electric guitars and acoustic guitars. Some people prefer thin picks, while others prefer thick picks. My dad and brother actually file the edges of their picks off so they are completely round and glide over the strings. I play with the rounded edge of my pick rather than the point that most people play with. Many musicians grab a handful of picks when they go to the music store, while some only buy one or two.

I remember going to the store with my mom when I was a child and watching her sort through her change purse to find the correct change for a purchase. She would find about five or six picks in her change purse and occasionally give one to the clerk by mistake. I always thought it was strange that she had so many picks in her change purse.

Today I find myself doing the same thing. I find picks in my wallet, in the clothes dryer, and all over the house. Just the other day, I was telling Mark that I couldn't find a single pick in the house and needed to buy more. Over the weekend, I cleaned my room and found about 15 picks in desk drawers and under furniture. I thought I had no picks, yet they were all around me; I just had to look for them.

We can find ourselves doing the same thing where thankfulness is concerned. We can constantly find something to complain about or need. We complain about the bills we have, the limited time we have, how small our closets are, and how we have no clothes that look good on us, but we neglect to see the little blessings that surround us. We need to do exactly what I did this weekend — clean out our closets for a spiritual inventory!

Do you have a house? The rent or mortgage may be high, but we aren't living in tents and fearing mosquito-borne illnesses. Do we have a load of homework to do with our children every night? Thank God we live in a country where our sons and daughters are free to learn and receive an education. Your clothes are getting too tight because suddenly the dryer is shrinking them? Ok, I won't go there! We do have clothes to wear, even if they aren't the most stylish. There's an old hymn that puts things in perspective:

> *"Count your blessings, name them one by one*
> *Count your blessings, see what God hath done*
> *Count your blessings, name them one by one*
> *Count your many blessings, see what God hath done!"*[39]

In every thing give thanks: for this is the will of God in Christ Jesus concerning you.
1 Thessalonians 5:18, KJV

THE SAFE ROOM

My friend Keith lives in northern Alabama and sends me updates of the weather there. He told me about some tornadoes that destroyed many homes in Cullman, Alabama and surrounding areas. One home that was destroyed belonged to the Crumbley family. When the tornado hit, the Crumbleys went into a "safe room" where they would remain until the storm passed by. Minutes later, the tornado came through and destroyed their home and cars, but they were safe inside the shelter. There was nothing left standing, except for the safe room!

I have heard of storm shelters, but never realized that safe rooms exist. Safe rooms are installed inside homes to provide protection from storms. This particular safe room had walls made of ¼-inch thick steel.

This story brings back memories from my childhood of storms that would pass through at night. My family would gather in the hallway, which was the safest place in the house. We would pray for safety and nervously start singing hymns. By the time we finished singing the first hymn, we were less fearful of the storm and had more faith that we would be protected.

Psalm 91:1-2 says, "Whoever dwells in the shelter of the Most High will rest in the shadow of the Almighty. I will say of the Lord, 'He is my refuge and my fortress, my God, in whom I trust'" (NIV).

Like the safe room that sheltered the Crumbley family from the tornado, we have a safe place from the storms and troubles of life that threaten us. We can't always stop the storms that we face, but we can trust that God is able to bring us through them. The Crumbley family just moved into a new house, and the same safe room that protected them in the storm was installed in their new home. We need to know that when things get rough, we always have a safe place to go. In His shelter we find peace, comfort, and rest when we need it the most!

But the men marvelled, saying, What manner of man is this, that even the winds and the sea obey him!
Matthew 8:27, KJV

320 POWER!

Today was "Take Your Daughter to Work Day," and I took Krista to work with me. After lunch, she went to visit her aunt at her office and got a full tour of the building. Afterwards, they went outside and watched as some ants carried a large crumb of food up a wall. Krista's aunt had her camera phone with her and sent me a picture of this amazing sight. Ants are simply fascinating! According to *Extension*, "Some ants are nearly blind. Rather than seeing, ants use their antennae to 'smell' food, to sense their surroundings, and to communicate with other ants."[40] Ants can lift about 20 times their own body weight. They use teamwork to lift a heavy object and are often seen carrying the object up a wall to their nests. The strength and brilliance of these insects is unheard of!

    I love the picture that my sister sent me of the ants, but what I love even more is the reminder that was attached. If you look closely at the file name, it is IMG952320. What's so amazing is the three numbers within — "320"! This has been my special number for a few years now because every time I see the numbers "320," whether on a cash register or a clock, I think of Ephesians

3:20, which says, "Now unto him that is able to do exceeding abundantly above all that we ask or think, according to the power that worketh in us..." (KJV). These words are more precious to me than solid gold.

God reminded me in this picture that it should be impossible for these tiny ants to lift this huge crumb, yet they have a power within that is able. There are many things that we should not be able to do, yet can from the power that is within us — the power of the Lord Almighty! Through Him we can do all things — even those that seem impossible!

Now unto him that is able to do exceeding abundantly above all that we ask or think, according to the power that worketh in us, Unto him be glory in the church by Christ Jesus throughout all ages, world without end.
Amen.
Ephesians 3:20-21, KJV

GEORGIA THUMPERS

While visiting my aunt in Havana, I walked out in the yard and was startled by a large grasshopper. I don't like bugs of any kind, so I quickly darted past the grasshopper, only to discover two more large grasshoppers in front of me. Starting to feel that a plague was developing before my very eyes, I quickly made my way to the car. The grasshoppers were just as afraid of me as I was of them. These large grasshoppers are called "Eastern Lubber" grasshoppers, or what southerners call "Georgia Thumpers."

As I reflected on the events of that day, God revealed something amazing to me. Although there was really nothing harmful about the grasshoppers, they still frightened me. Even if they could not harm me, I could certainly harm myself while trying to get away from them.

I immediately thought of the Bible story involving the spies that were sent into the land of Canaan. In this story, the spies came back with a cluster of grapes so large that it had to be carried on a pole between two men. After showing the fruit to Moses, the spies reported that, although Canaan was a great land flowing with milk and honey, the giants in the land were stronger than they were. The King James Version of scripture says, "And there we saw the giants, the sons of Anak, which come of the giants: and we were in our own sight as grasshoppers, and so we were in their sight" (Numbers 13:33, KJV). Four words caught my attention — "*in our own sight.*"

God revealed to me a desire that he had placed on my heart recently and that I was like the spies that I read about. I was already defeated — *in my own sight*, but according to God's Word, "I can do all things through Christ who strengtheneth me" (Philippians 4:13, KJV).

For with God nothing shall be impossible.
Luke 1:37, KJV

LOCKED DOOR!

A few years ago, we bought Krista a trampoline for her birthday. She enjoyed playing on the trampoline for only a week or two and never played on it again. The trampoline just collected pine straw and pollen and hasn't been used since. We decided to sell the trampoline so that another family could enjoy it and we could have more room in our yard.

A family called the second day that it was advertised and came to pick it up. When they arrived, their boys were very excited. One boy was excited about taking the trampoline home, while the other boy was excited — *about my daughter!* Krista picked up on his enthusiasm and ran inside to get away from him. It apparently didn't stop the boy because soon he was looking through the glass door and begging her to let him in. I heard him make every excuse about why he needed to come in, but Krista locked the door and ignored his pleas. Her daddy hopes that she reacts this way with boys for years to come!

We have many decisions in life as to which doors to open and close. There is a famous painting by Holman Hunt, which portrays Jesus knocking at a door. *Hearttalks.com* tells us, "When Holman Hunt had completed his famous picture of Jesus standing at the door with a lighted lantern, he showed it to a friend. The friend told him that he had made a serious mistake: he had forgotten to put a latch on the door. 'No,' the artist replied, 'that is the way it should be. You see, the latch is on the inside.' If you would have Christ come into your heart you must open the door yourself."[41]

Like Krista, we all have a decision to either open the door and let the Lord come into our hearts, or to simply lock the door and leave him out. We also have to decide to not just let him in, but to give him the keys to our hearts! I usually close my bedroom door if my room isn't quite clean enough for company to see. Thankfully, Jesus is not intimidated by my messy heart. He will not be scared away. Instead, he will help clean up if we will let Him!

Behold, I stand at the door, and knock: if any man hear my voice, and open the door, I will come in to him, and will sup with him, and he with me.
Revelation 3:20, KJV

THE COIN JEWELRY

Krista, my sister, and I went to an arts and crafts event where vendors displayed their unique, handcrafted items. We enjoyed the beautiful arts and crafts, but our favorite booth had a display of ordinary coins and silverware that were made into beautiful jewelry creations.

We found it difficult to decide which items to purchase because there were so many beautiful pieces to choose from, but we left with necklaces made from quarters, and earrings made from dimes. Krista was proud that her earrings were shinier than mine because her dimes were from 2002 and mine were from 1976. When I came home, I was excited to tell my friend about the great deal I'd gotten on the dime earrings. "I only paid $10 for that pair of earrings!" She raised an eyebrow and said, "You paid $10 for something worth 20 cents?" All of a sudden, I realized that although I value my beautiful earrings, she had a point. In reality, my treasured earrings were still only worth 20 cents!

As I proudly wear my new dime earrings bearing the year I was born, I realize that we put a value on things every day and don't realize it. Judas Iscariot put a value on his relationship with Christ when he betrayed Him for 30 pieces of silver. It is estimated that 30 pieces of silver was worth the price of a slave, or about 4 months' pay. This must have seemed of great value to Judas, yet in reality was worth so little eternally!

How great Christ's sacrifice was for us! Do we value Him? Until 1965, coin sizes were based on their worth. The average dime contained 90% silver and 10% copper. Just because the dime was smaller in size did not mean it was worth less.

According to *Wikipedia,* "With the passage of the Coinage Act of 1965, the dime's silver content was removed. Dimes from 1965 to the present are composed of outer layers of 75 percent copper and 25 percent nickel, bonded to a pure copper core."[42]

After the silver dimes began to disappear from circulation, they were sought after by collectors. What once was of great value now seemed priceless, yet hard to obtain. We also need to appreciate the things that are of value while we can still treasure them. Seek God while He may be found. Enjoy time with our families while we have them. Appreciate our jobs because we may find ourselves without one someday. Sometimes it's the small things in life that are most valuable!

Lay not up for yourselves treasures upon earth, where moth and rust doth corrupt, and where thieves break through and steal: But lay up for yourselves treasures in heaven, where neither moth nor rust doth corrupt, and where thieves do not break through nor steal: For where your treasure is, there will your heart be also.
Matthew 6:19-21, KJV

THE GYM MEMBERSHIP

I noticed a familiar tag hanging from my keychain, and I specifically remember the day that I received the tag. I was so displeased with the photograph that was printed on it — *my* photograph! This tag was my gym membership access card. I attended that gym faithfully for many months until little obligations popped up here and there. I missed one aerobics class, then another, until I no longer went. Months passed and I have put on a pound here and there. I now look at this membership access tag and realize that I don't even have a contract with this gym and am certainly not feeling the benefits of being physically fit that a membership could provide. It's time to remove the tag until I join again.

We carry many tags or labels in life — mother, father, employee, student, etc. Some of us carry the "Christian" label, but like my gym membership access card, it is only a label — a source of identity with none of the benefits associated with it.

We don't depend on God to be our strength in difficult times and often go days without praying. We don't offer praise for the good things, but complain about the bad. We carry heavy loads and don't allow God to help us bear the weight. Don't just be a card-carrying Christian, but exercise spiritual discipline daily.

Bless the Lord, O my soul, and forget not all his benefits: Who forgiveth all thine iniquities; who healeth all thy diseases; Who redeemeth thy life from destruction; who crowneth thee with lovingkindness and tender mercies; Who satisfieth thy mouth with good things; so that thy youth is renewed like the eagle's.
Psalm 103:2-5, KJV

R.I.P., RED!

A few years ago, I bought a sporty red station wagon from California and had it shipped to my home in Georgia. I cringe to even call it a station wagon because it was way too sporty to be called a station wagon; it was a sports wagon!

I live in a fairly small city, and people were constantly telling me where they had seen my car. The transmission went out last week, and when I traded "Red" in on another car, the salesman told me that he had seen my car all over Thomasville and Tallahassee. We traded Red in on a newer model car, which would be more economical. The new car is comfortable and will definitely be a reliable vehicle based on all the reviews, but today I realized one thing that I would truly miss about Red — she certainly knew how to stand out in a crowd!

As I walked out into the parking lot to find my new car, I realized that I couldn't tell that car apart from any other car in the parking lot. This may be a little frustrating because I can never remember where I park! As I searched for my new car in the crowded parking lot, I wondered if I stand out like Red. As a Christian, do I seem different, or do I simply blend in like my new car? Do people see me and say, "There is something different about that girl"? Do I show that I'm a Jesus-lover, or do I seem as just another person in the world — trying to make it through another day? Do I show that I have extreme faith even when I'm tempted not to? Do I show love to people whom others pass by? R.I.P., Red! You are gone, but not forgotten!

And be not conformed to this world: but be ye transformed by the renewing of your mind, that ye may prove what is that good, and acceptable, and perfect, will of God.
(Romans 12:2, KJV)

THE OPEN BOOK TEST

Krista was telling me about a test that she had to take at school. She wasn't worried about the test because it was an open-book test, meaning that she was allowed to use her study guide to answer the questions.

Just this week, I had to take a test at work and was also allowed to use my study guide to aid in the test. Although many of the questions seemed like they required only a little common sense, many would have been marked wrong if I had gone with what seemed right. It suddenly occurred to me that life is nothing more than an open book test.

We face many tests and challenges in life — whether making tough choices, or dealing with life's heartaches. We can respond with what may seem like a common sense answer, but like the test that I took, a common sense answer could be the wrong answer! In this test called "life," God gives us some guides to follow — the Bible and the Holy Spirit. These guides will comfort us and lead us in the way we should go if we will follow. Sometimes God's leading may seem uncommon and somewhat unfamiliar, but He is the way, and only He has the answers to life's tests.

Jesus saith unto him, I am the way, the truth, and the life: no man cometh unto the Father, but by me.
John 14:6, KJV

THE EGG SALAD MESS

My church family had the great privilege of showing love to a family that lost a loved one, by providing a meal for the family after the funeral. I had plans to bring a container of deviled eggs. After all, deviled eggs were easy to make, and who doesn't love deviled eggs, right? I went to the store early that morning and ran into a friend who suggested that I just make egg salad instead of deviled eggs because it would be easier, but I wanted to make deviled eggs. I love the uniqueness of deviled eggs and how they have their own little enclosures. They are easy to grab and no mess is involved. I boiled the eggs, soaked them in cold water, and started peeling them, but then something disastrous happened — part of the egg whites peeled right off with the shell. I had created a fine mess! I suddenly remembered my friend's suggestion about the egg salad and decided that egg salad was my best option at this point. I shamefully brought my pathetic egg salad to the family reception and waited for the crowd to arrive. *Who is going to eat egg salad with so many other goodies on the table?* The crowd arrived and the egg salad was almost gone! At that time, one of the family members told me how much he loves egg salad. It made me feel good to know that something that I considered such a mess turned out to be a comfort food.

I saw a church sign while driving that said, "God can turn a mess into a message!" I truly believe this. I have been in situations that seemed like an absolute disaster at the time and later saw God's fingerprints all over it and realized that He had been there with a plan in the midst of the mess. Surely He doesn't plan for bad things to happen, but there is nothing that God cannot use. Even in tragedy,

God has a plan to turn suffering into something beautiful. God loves us so much! Matthew 10:29-31 says, "Are not two sparrows sold for a penny? Yet not one of them will fall to the ground outside your Father's care. And even the very hairs of your head are all numbered. So don't be afraid; you are worth more than many sparrows" (NIV). The death of our Lord and Savior seemed to end in tragedy, but that tragedy was transformed into triumph. He could have saved Himself, but instead, His death created abundant life for us. I am thankful that the Christ babe came to a messy world to be our Message. Let God take whatever mess you are going through and turn it into a message.

Are not two sparrows sold for a penny? Yet not one of them will fall to the ground outside your Father's care. And even the very hairs of your head are all numbered. So don't be afraid; you are worth more than many sparrows.
Matthew 10:29-31, NIV

LOVE BUG SEASON

It is love bug season in Florida, and I am at the gas station, watching five different people around me wash bugs off of their windshields. Love bug season comes twice a year in Florida, and motorists must constantly scrub the love bugs from their cars. When a love bug splatters onto the car, it releases an acid that can seem like glue. If the love bug "glue" isn't removed, it may not only limit the driver's vision, but can also damage the car's paint and can even make the engine overheat! The longer a splattered love bug remains attached, the harder it is to clean off. It isn't easy to scrape off the bugs, but is definitely necessary.

I feel like a love bug stuck to the car window at times. I can often allow myself to get stuck in a comfort zone. To say that I don't like change is an understatement! I would much rather stick with what I know is comfortable than to venture out and face the unknown, but I know that I can become like that love bug on the windshield of my car.

God knows the path I should take, and in order for His will to be done, I must sometimes let go and let Him clear away the things that are limiting His vision for my life. If I will just be the passenger on this ride, He will take me where I need to go.

Trust in the Lord with all thine heart; and lean not unto thine own understanding. In all thy ways acknowledge him, and he shall direct thy paths.
Proverbs 3:5-6, KJV

IN THE PALM OF HIS HAND

My mom recently told me a heart-wrenching story that was somewhat sad, yet humorous and comforting. She was sitting inside her house when she suddenly heard a loud thump. In the backyard, she discovered a helpless bird lying on the ground. There was an imprint of a bird on the window, and she realized that the bird had flown into the window and injured itself. She picked up the bird and watched helplessly as it gasped and died in her hand. "I even tried to pump his little chest to give him CPR," she said. That made me laugh a little, and I jokingly asked her if she gave the bird mouth to mouth.

My mom loves to sit at her window and watch the birds eat and play. It caused her great pain to see her feathered friend die because she would do anything to keep her birds safe.

This story reminded me of how God sees us. Just as my mom saw the bird, God sees us when we are well and when we fall. Matthew 10:29-31 says, "Are not two sparrows sold for a farthing? and one of them shall not fall on the ground without your Father. But the very hairs of your head are all numbered. Fear ye not therefore, ye are of more value than many sparrows" (KJV).

What this version doesn't tell you is that a "farthing" is equivalent to less than a penny! Our Father, who owns the cattle on a thousand hills, cares about a bird that is worth less than a penny! Psalm 50:10-11 says, "For every beast of the forest is mine, and the cattle upon a thousand hills. I know all the fowls of the mountains: and the wild beasts of the field are mine" (KJV).

As I imagine my mom holding the little bird in the palm of her hand and trying to give it life again, I have a beautiful image of what John 10:28 must look like. "And I give unto them eternal life; and they shall never perish, neither shall any man pluck them out of my hand" (KJV). When we accept Christ into our hearts, we are given the promise of eternal life which cannot be taken from us — even in death. Just as this little bird was held and loved, God holds us in the palm of His hand, and no one can remove us from His care. When you see the birds today, remember how He loves them, but also remember how much more valuable you are to Him.

And I give unto them eternal life; and they shall never perish, neither shall any man pluck them out of my hand.
John 10:28, KJV

THE COWBELL

I loved to play outside when I was young. Unlike today's generation, children would come home after school to play with their baby dolls and miniature cars. My daddy made a playhouse for me out of a refrigerator box one time. He cut holes in the box and transformed it into a house with windows and doors. It even had a pretend kitchen where I made delicious cakes and pies for my friends. I would play outdoors until my mom called me in at dinner time. If I was too far away and couldn't hear her voice, she would ring the cowbell. I knew that the cowbell meant it was time to come home — and fast! My mom still has that cowbell today. That cowbell was used to guide us home at night, but cowbells were originally used to aid shepherds in keeping track of livestock. The bell was placed on the animal's neck, and each herd had its own particular type of bell. The shepherd knew which sound belonged to each herd and was aware if the animals strayed from the rest of the herd, or if the animal was attacked by another animal.

The Bible tells us in Isaiah 53:6, "We all, like sheep, have gone astray, each of us has turned to our own way..." (NIV). In Luke 15:4-7, Jesus tells gives a parable, "Suppose one of you has a hundred sheep and loses one of them. Doesn't he leave the ninety-nine in the open country and go after the lost sheep until he finds it? And when he finds it, he joyfully puts it on his shoulders and goes home. Then he calls his friends and neighbors together and says, 'Rejoice with me; I have found my lost sheep'" (NIV). I have always loved the famous picture of Jesus carrying the lost sheep on His shoulders.

At times, I feel that I have lost my way, whether I am straying spiritually, or weary and worn from the heaviness of life. Jesus knows exactly where we are and is ready and willing to draw us back and carry our heavy loads on His strong shoulders if we will let him. Like the cowbell that my mom rang, He is calling "Come home!"

But the father said to his servants, Bring forth the best robe, and put it on him; and put a ring on his hand, and shoes on his feet: And bring hither the fatted calf, and kill it; and let us eat, and be merry: For this my son was dead, and is alive again; he was lost, and is found. And they began to be merry.
Luke 15:22-24, KJV

GERALDO'S NEW HOME

BY KRISTA PIKE (AGE 10)

A couple days ago, I asked daddy if I could have a pet fish. He was quiet at first, but then he said if I was good for a week he would get me a Betta fish. We finally went to the pet store to get my fish. As soon as we walked in, we saw all kinds of colorful fish. I thought it would be hard to choose which one I wanted because there were so many beautiful fish. Finally, I found one that I wanted. The fish that I got was blue and red and had a big frown on its face. When we checked out, the lady at the pet store gave us a pamphlet that told us all of the things we needed to know about the fish. When we got to the car, my daddy asked me what we should name the fish. After a few minutes he had a suggestion. "How about Esmeralda?" he asked. "Ok," I said. Once we got home, I started reading the pamphlet and realized that the fish was a boy, so I named him Geraldo.

When we first got Geraldo, he was in a tiny container that was hardly big enough for him to swim. My mama and I went to the store and got him a new fish bowl, some blue, shiny water rocks, and a pretty green plant. When we got home from the store, we put the rocks and the plant inside the fish bowl and sat it next to Geraldo. He was staring at his new fish bowl all night. I think he was unhappy in his little container and excited about moving into his new home. The next morning, my daddy scooped up Geraldo with a measuring cup and put him in his new fish bowl. Once Geraldo got in his new fish bowl, he started swimming around. The Bible says in Philippians 3:20-21, "But our citizenship is in heaven. And we eagerly await a Savior from there, the Lord Jesus Christ, who, by the power that enables him to bring everything under his control, will transform our lowly bodies so that they will be like his glorious body" (NIV). Geraldo was looking forward to being in his new home like we are looking forward to heaven!

CONCLUSION

In conclusion, I hope you enjoyed the stories in this book, but I sincerely hope that it has compelled you to look for God in the small things. Think about the event that you remember most in your day. It may be something you saw in nature, or something that a relative or friend did. Then ask yourself if there can be a bigger picture. Can it relate to a particular scripture, or to a particular characteristic of the Lord? I would love to hear your stories. You can contact me at writtenintheskies320@gmail.com

In Him,

Amy

WORKS CITED

[1] Asbury-Oliver, Suzanne. "Skywriting...from Olivers Flying Circus." *Skywriting...from Olivers Flying Circus*. Olivers Flying Circus, n.d. Web. 29 Oct. 2013. www.skywriter.info/NASM%20PEPSI%20DOC.pdf

[2] Lehman, Frederick M., comp. "The Love of God.", 1917, Public Domain.

[3] "Dictionary, Encyclopedia and Thesaurus." *The Free Dictionary*. Farlex, n.d. Web. 27 Oct. 2013. www.thefreedictionary.com/salvage.

[4] "Wit and Wisdom." *PBS*. PBS, n.d. Web. 27 Oct. 2013.

[5] "'A Most Awkward, Ridiculous Appearance': Benjamin Franklin Enters Philadelphia." *'A Most Awkward, Ridiculous Appearance': Benjamin Franklin Enters Philadelphia"*. History Matters, n.d. Web. 27 Oct. 2013. historymatters.gmu.edu/d/5823

[6] "'Never Be Afraid to Trust an Unknown Future to a Known God.'" *Goodreads*. Goodreads, n.d. Web. 09 Nov. 2013. www.goodreads.com/quotes/70125-never-be-afraid-to-trust-an-unknown-future-to-a

[7] "Corrie Ten Boom." *Wikipedia*. Wikipedia, n.d. Web. 29 Oct. 2013. < en.wikipedia.org/wiki/Corrie_ten_Boom

[8] "This Is What the past Is For! Every Experience God Gives Us, Every Person He Puts in Our Lives Is the Perfect Preparation for the Future That Only He Can See". *Goodreads*. Goodreads, n.d. Web. 09 Nov. 2013. www.goodreads.com/quotes/94188-this-is-what-the-past-is-for-every-experience-god

[9] Mayo Clinic. "Did You Know?" *Interesting Facts about Blood Donation*. Mayo Clinic, n.d. Web. 22 Oct. 2013. www.mayoclinic.org/donate-blood-rst/know.html

[10] Donlan, Francesca. "Fla. Blood donor earns world record." *USATODAY.COM*. USATODAY.COM, 06 Aug. 2011. Web. 22 Oct. 2013. usatoday30.usatoday.com/news/nation/2011-08-06-blood-donation-record_n.htm

[11] Lowry, Robert, comp. Nothing But the Blood." 1876., Public Domain.

[12] Branham, Marc. "How and Why Do Fireflies Light Up?" *How and Why Do Fireflies Light Up?: Scientific American*. Scientific American, 05 Sept. 2005. Web. 27 Oct. 2013. www.scientificamerican.com/article.cfm?id=how-and-why-do-fireflies

[13] "Firefly Bioluminescence." *Firefly Bioluminescence -*. Wikidot, 09 Feb. 2008. Web. 29 Nov. 2013.

[14] "Information OnThe Firefly - Lightning Bug Facts - Kemana Perginya Kelip-Kelip." *Kemana Perginya Kelip-Kelip*. Kemana Perginya Kelip-Kelip, 19 Jan. 2011. Web. 28 Oct. 2013. kelipkelip.weebly.com/2/post/2011/01/information-onthe-firefly-lightning-bug-facts.html

[15] "Fervor." *Merriam-Webster*. Merriam-Webster, n.d. Web. 11 Nov. 2013. www.merriam-webster.com/dictionary/fervor

[16] "Zeal." *Merriam-Webster*. Merriam-Webster, n.d. Web.

11 Nov. 2013. www.merriam-webster.com/dictionary/zeal?show=0

[17] "Stone Mountain Park - Atlanta's Walk-Up Mountain Hiking Trail." *Stone Mountain Park - Atlanta's Walk-Up Mountain Hiking Trail.* Stone Mountain Park, n.d. Web. 22 Oct. 2013. www.stonemountainpark.com/activities/recreation-golf/Walk-Up-Trail-to-Top-of-Stone-Mountain.aspx

[18] "Stone Mountain Park - Confederate Memorial Carving." *Stone Mountain Park - Confederate Memorial Carving.* Stone Mountain Park, n.d. Web. 26 Oct. 2013. www.stonemountainpark.com/activities/history-nature/Confederate-Memorial-Carving.aspx

[19] "Monarch Viceroy Mimicry." *Henderson State University.* Henderson State University. Web 26 Oct. 2013. www.hsu.edu/pictures.aspx?id=1989

[20] Widmeyer, Charles B., comp. "Come and Dine.", 1907, Public Domain.

[21] Miles, C. Austin, comp. "In the Garden.", 1912., Public Domain.

[22] Britton, Dave, Ph.D. "Cicadas: Superfamily Cicadoidea - Australian Museum." *Cicadas: Superfamily Cicadoidea - Australian Museum.* Austrailian Museum, 19 Mar. 2012. Web. 26 Oct. 2013. australianmuseum.net.au/Cicadas-Superfamily-Cicadoidea

[23] "How Do Oysters Make Pearls?" *HowStuffWorks.*

HowStuffWorks, n.d. Web. 11 Nov. 2013.
science.howstuffworks.com/zoology/question630.htm

[24] "The Big Oak and Big Oak Cam." *Thomasville Visitor's Center*. Thomasville Visitor's Center, n.d. Web. 26 Oct. 2013.
www.thomasvillega.com/Content/Default/8/40/15/thomasville-visitor's-center/visit-us/attractions.html

[25] Ibid.

[26] "Liberty Bell Center." *National Park Service*. National Park Service, 17 Oct. 2013. Web. 28 Oct. 2013.
www.nps.gov/inde/liberty-bell-center.htm

[27] "Symphony No. 9 (Beethoven)." *Wikipedia*. Wikimedia Foundation, 24 Oct. 2013. Web. 28 Oct. 2013.
en.wikipedia.org/wiki/Symphony_No._9_(Beethoven)

[28] Ibid.

[29] Ibid.

[30] Fowler, E. 2011. "Pavo cristatus" (On-line), Animal Diversity Web. Accessed October 26, 2013 at animaldiversity.ummz.umich.edu/accounts/Pavo_cristatus

[31] "The PubWire - Aesop's Fables." *The PubWire*. The PubWire, n.d. Web. 28 Oct. 2013.
www.pubwire.com/DownloadDocs/AFABLES.PDF

[32] "General Robert E. Lee's War-Horses, Traveller And Lucy Long." *General Robert E. Lee's War-Horses, Traveller And Lucy Long*. Civilwarhome.com, n.d. Web. 26 Oct. 2013.

www.civilwarhome.com/leeshorses.htm

[33] "Frogs and toads." WelcomeWildlife.com. Welcome Wildlife.com. Web. 26 Oct. 2013. www.welcomewildlife.com/?folder=pages/urban%20wildlife/amphibians

[34] "Oboe." *Wikipedia*. Wikimedia Foundation, 24 Oct. 2013. Web. 26 Oct. 2013. en.wikipedia.org/wiki/Oboe

[35] "Tetelestai." *Men of Destiny*. Men of Destiny, n.d. Web. 26 Oct. 2013. www.menofdestiny.com/encounter-module-tetelestai.html

[36] "Michelangelo Paints the Sistine Chapel," EyeWitness to History, www.eyewitnesstohistory.com (2005). www.eyewitnesstohistory.com/michelangelo.htm

[37] Looney Tunes and Merrie Melodies Films. Warner Bros. Entertainment, Inc. (1940-1949).

[38] "Simon." *Wikipedia*. Wikimedia Foundation, 21 Oct. 2013. Web. 26 Oct. 2013. en.wikipedia.org/wiki/Simon

[39] Oatman, Johnson, Jr., comp. "Count Your Blessings.", 1987., Public Domain.

[40] "Fire Ant Physiques." *EXtension*. EXtension, 2013. Web. 26 Oct. 2013. www.extension.org/pages/15937/fire-ant-physiques#.UoErNHDvuhE

[41] "Christ At The Door." *Heart-talks.com*. Heart-talks.com. Web. 26 Oct. 2013. www.heart-talks.com/christatdoor.html

[42] "Dime (United States Coin)." *Wikipedia*. Wikimedia Foundation, 29 Oct. 2013. Web. 29 Oct. 2013. en.wikipedia.org/wiki/Coins_of_the_United_States_dollar

Made in the USA
Charleston, SC
01 December 2014